Surviving a 'New Norm'
created by
Loss & Bereavement:
Moving from Trauma to Insight

By
Wendy Wren

A CIP record for this title is available from the British Library.
Printed in the United Kingdom
First printed, 2021

ISBN: 978-1838369118 (paperback)

Published by
The Self Publishing Studio

This book is dedicated to my late father, George, who taught me about the effects of trauma and hidden, entrenched pain.

It is also dedicated to the brave people who choose to talk about their losses. The dead survive in our memories and live within our conversations.

———

"I sat with my anger long enough, until she told me her real name was grief."

Cruse Bereavement Care

———

Foreword

It takes an awful lot of courage to write such a book. Writing can often feel like bearing your heart and soul in print. Presenting a history of your life in such a way as to illustrate the development of trauma and the impact of bereavement, is both poignant and heartfelt.

We know from much research, professional insight and feedback from bereaved people, that the telling of one's story is vital. The 'bearing witness' to events, the life and death of those who are no longer with us in body, and the impact of the loss, helps us develop an understanding of what this all means. How we derive meaning from the death can then have a profound effect on how we live with that loss.

Through this personal account, Wendy has illustrated how our history, our physical selves, our emotional and psychological wellbeing, our thought processes, and our social connectedness, are all linked together. Death impacts on all of these elements, and trauma does too. The echoes of traumatic encounters often reverberate through our lives, from the times of the trauma to the present day.

Yet, Wendy also paints a picture of where hope can lie. How forming reparative relationships can be healing. How commitment and compassion can win through. And how, although it is often painful and requires great tenacity, self-reflection and the seeking of support can also reap rewards. It is possible, albeit a great challenge, to use what we have experienced to learn and to reach an understanding of how we want life to be. The aspiration for us all, to be operating and responding at the confluent level, is a very compelling one.

We are grateful for this book. Its content and the strategies within will be valuable to many. We are also grateful for Wendy's kind donation of the royalties of this book to Cruse, alongside the Cavernoma Alliance. This will help us support many more people who are bereaved.

Andy Langford
Clinical Director, Cruse Bereavement Care

If this book has been a rallying call for you, you may decide you want to help too, by volunteering at Cruse. If that is the case, you would be most welcome to contact us:
www.cruse.org.uk

Acknowledgements

Thank you to my husband Steve who, for 30 years, has been my dependable rock. If anyone can cope with a crisis, Steve can. To my children, Max and Ruby-Rose, who make me laugh every day. I have many best friends, all much appreciated, but special thanks to Elaine, Susan, Amrit, Kay, Kelley, Gela, Jan, Juana, Katherine, Sally and Sarah-Jane, who were all able to 'hear my story' and stick with it. To my mother, who is an amazing grandma and is a testament to positivity and healing. Also, a heartfelt thank you to my two resilient sisters, Yonnie and Pam-ella – we are like triplets! To my brother Dave who, despite his learning disability, has taught me how to be a better human being.

To my late father who, despite his own trauma, had love in his heart and was taken too soon. To my present GP, Dr Fernando, for his unwavering support, who took away my bereavement anger, without even realising it – thank you.

To the many other good people who I have met on my medical journey, who've taught me about humanity and the importance of listening. To the Chief Executive of my local Hampshire hospital, who is actively listening and responding to her staff and patients. Thank you for sorting out my delayed appointments.

To the alternative therapists who played a big part in helping me to manage my symptoms, whilst also making me laugh and keeping me emotionally well: my acupuncturist, Daren Oliver, my reflexologist, Tracey Wakely, my beauty therapists, Sobia Razzaq and Emma Kennedy and my deep tissue therapist, Sandra Jobges. Each one of you taught me something different about life and this helped me to heal.

Also, thanks to the 'Cavernoma Alliance' in the UK and the US, who provide an extraordinary Facebook support network for people suffering from brain cavernomas. A huge amount of people benefit from your site and your insight. Thank you to both the leaders and your members. Thank you also to 'Cruse Bereavement Care' for your daily dedication to trauma recovery, active listening and support. Thank you to my consultant occupational physician who 'understood' my symptoms and my issues of non-functionality, within a two-hour conversation. Some people do just 'get it' and there is a lot of validation in that.

Appreciation to Gillian who, due to my peripheral neuropathy, typed up my manuscript. Without her input, this book would never have been written up.

Thank you to the Nexus Campus, Cornwall and to Farnborough Sixth Form College, for your outstanding support to the children and young people during the Covid-19 crisis.

Thank you to my copywriter, Pru, who edited the journey alongside me, via Zoom, to protect my fingertips and who had the emotional resilience to help me articulate my story; I could not have asked for more.

To my publisher, Paul, who managed the methodical publishing process with direction and super efficiency. To Malcolm, for designing the book cover and for enthusiastically sticking with my idea.

We currently live in the era of the Covid-19 pandemic. Thank you to the government, the local support groups and the medical world who battle onwards regardless. A special thank you to Chris Whitty and his colleagues, who always understood the relationship and balance between health and trauma. To Joe Biden, who understands the concept of confluence and the ideals of better relationships, improved social structures and a harmonious balance with the natural world.

Contents

Surviving a 'New Norm'

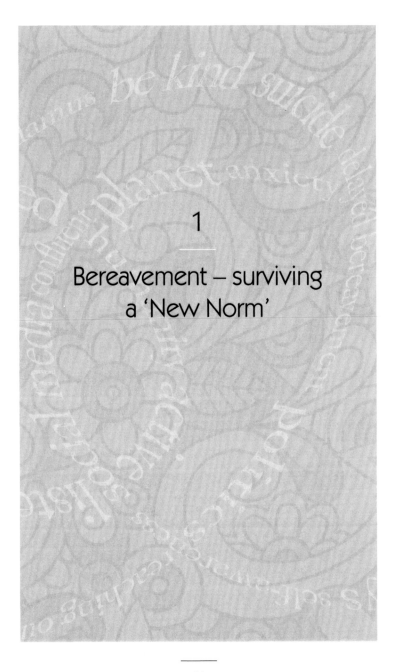

1

Bereavement – surviving a 'New Norm'

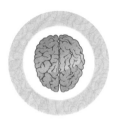

How do we adjust to the 'new norm' following loss? There is no specific end date for closure on bereavement or clear stages of loss. Yes, we do tend to have certain expectations. These expectations can put individuals under pressure, especially when they are not feeling 'better'. How do we survive loss and reach out to others? How does loss exacerbate difficult relationships? How can we understand mental distress sufficiently to truly reach out to others? How can we understand and connect better as human beings?

This book explores the link between trauma, bereavement and ill health. It explores the role of family and what happens when relationships are lacking. It provides a toolkit to assist people to heal and gain better insight, to themselves and others.

It pulls apart the socio-economic, the sociological and psychological development of different people and how early experiences inform our future adult personalities and exchanges. It explores upbringing, schooling and relationships in detail and provides insights into the trauma and bereavement relationship. The book unravels the theme of trauma, for rich and poor, in the context of mental wellbeing, and proposes insight and fresh ideologies for a new way of being. The intention is that this will enable readers to be 'partners' in bereavement understanding, good mental health and wellbeing.

It differentiates between the trajectory of human beings. There are those who are high achievers and then there are those who are often 'outbursting' and always on the edge of not coping. Where do these trajectories stem from and how can we capture, in our hearts, both extremes of this dichotomy? How do we explore our mixture of both extremes?

All cognitive adults indeed have aspects of both trajectories and, in understanding the brain, our early experiences, relationships, trauma-induced pain, good mental health and support, we can assess 'where we are' in the world and how we can connect better with each other. Terminologies around the subject of bereavement are not enough on their own, they require a deeper level of understanding. This endeavour, for further insight, is of course combined with the good work of established charities of support, which sit alongside such terms. Every loss and experience is unique but a general understanding of trauma and health can assist many individuals. Even if you do not have health difficulties, exploring emotional trauma should still help, as will the strategies such as coping, functioning, parenting (if appropriate), connecting and healing.

Gender, identity, race, wealth, sexuality and poverty all partly disadvantage people, both males and females, and we have never seen this more starkly than during the Covid-19 crisis. Whilst the focus of this book is on bereavement, ill health and trauma, these sociological areas clearly do have a disproportionate effect on trauma and this book should be read in that context. I aspire to a place in society where human beings earn equal respect and relationships are more 'confluent'. Confluent relationships serve to meet the emotional needs of all bereaved participants and exist for the benefit of good mental health, arranged in a symmetrical, flowing way. Covid-19 has dramatically broken down county and country borders and has demonstrated that perhaps we are all ultimately grieving citizens of the world.

The book firstly explores my childhood which sets the scene

---

around bereavement and trauma. It will be different to your childhood experience but we all have similarities and differences, as we face our own human endeavours. The focus on me should enable readers to understand later on why and how I respond in certain ways with regard to my emotions, health and relationships. It offers a storyline, or 'flow', that is both personal and political.

Then I talk about my health journey, which was partly caused and exacerbated by multiple bereavements. I have focused mainly on health because I believe that early trauma, health and relationships are unavoidably entwined.

I go on to explore the treatment of people in society and the reasons why people behave as they do. I examine the theories around trauma, which I find useful in understanding the human endeavour to gain insight. The type of themes that pop up for others are often around alcohol misuse, self-medication, poor parenting, sibling rivalry, self-harm, resentment, favouritism, rejection, probate, jealousy, regret… the list is endless. I explore the skills and practical solutions, set out as strategies, which would work in all cultural contexts.

This leads us to discover new ways to move forward regarding how we can be kinder, to ourselves and to the bereaved.

To conclude, I consolidate what we have learnt throughout the journey. Understanding bereavement trauma is central to moving forwards in a more manageable way. By becoming more self-aware, individuals are able to get the best out of their relationships. Bereavements can lead us all to a 'new norm' and I sincerely hope that this book will enable you to understand your feelings better and in turn, be able to reach out and help others.

"Healing doesn't have to look magical or pretty. Real healing is hard, exhausting and draining. Let yourself go through it. Don't try to paint it as anything other than what it is. Be there for yourself with no judgement."

Audrey Kitching

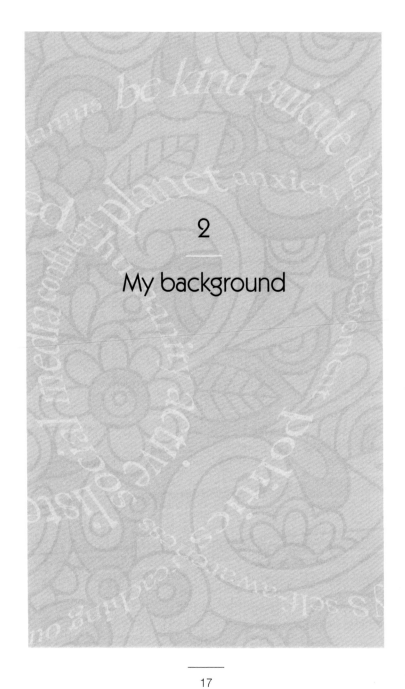

2

My background

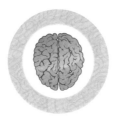

My background is here to set the scene of what would be quite normal to people suffering various forms of trauma. I have used my own story so that the reader can gain insight into what makes some people 'chaotic adults'. This may resonate but it does not have to. It is more to pave the way and you certainly do not have to endure 'bad' experiences to be emphatic but, in one way or another, we have all faced our own traumas or demons. This book is not a competition around whose negative experience is felt most.

When I was a younger adult, I would often play down my early experiences, believing that they would just be too much to be heard or too 'bad' to be believed. I have found as I have opened up more that people are more than willing to listen, now more than ever. Sometimes we must take a 'risk' on what we share with other people. From being a really shy (elective mute) young schoolgirl, I have, as an adult, found my voice.

My story begins with suicide. My maternal grandfather took his own life in 1968. He was found floating in the lake of the Royal Military Academy, Sandhurst. The coroner's report makes for quite harrowing reading. Immediately after his suicide, my mother became sick with anguish, understandably, and her contraceptive pill stopped working, due to her anxiety and stress. I was conceived and then born in January 1969. My very birth was defined by suicide: if the suicide had not happened, I would not be here.

There is no rosy way around it; for all the positive thinking, my life is partly defined by tragedy. My maternal grandmother died almost one year to the day later. I was born whilst my mother was grieving and I can only imagine that her pregnancy must have been a tragic time – perhaps a time where she was simply in survival mode. At a few months old, when I was just a little baby, my mother had lost her mother. I cannot remember a time in my life that I wasn't highly aware of my extreme entrance into the world. My mother had no siblings, so she was the end of the line.

My father, chronically shy like my mother, was emotionally trapped. His stress level was zero so there was no 'escalator' to pull back from: he could go from calm to angry in just one second. As an adult, I have worked with young offenders and I've never met another individual who takes so long to de-escalate as my father did. He had lost his mother when he was six and then lost his sister to leukaemia a couple of years later. I have been to the graveside of this little girl and I imagine that she must have felt very lost without her mother. A further sister of my father's died in young adulthood. So George (as we called my father) was himself traumatised by multiple and immediate family bereavements.

Laughter was always present around my siblings, but laughter and expression had to be hushed somewhat so as not to upset anyone. My parents didn't smile very often: they were intrinsically saddened by tragedy and were emotionally limited from the world around them. I still laugh, even whilst rolling around uncontrollably, with little sound, which my own daughter finds hilarious. My laughter has been partly silenced and I am intrinsically shy, but I have worked on my skills over the years to present as less shy than I am.

My early childhood memories are a paradox of both emotional distress and happy times. My first memory is of my father chasing me around the garden with a scythe, threatening to slice my head off. This was not a dark childhood game, it was real. Our garden was fairly large and my parents loved gardening. It was perhaps their only 'therapy', for gardens provide much more than we ever give, even to the most dedicated of gardeners. Part of our garden was lawn, with a criss-cross of paths and fruit trees. I diagonally dodged my father as he held the scythe above his head that day. I know I could have died, I saw it in his eyes. I cannot even remember what I had done 'wrong'.

We were not allowed to speak very much or express our views. I remember being scalded very badly one day when we had been out visiting 'Nana', who wasn't actually our grandma but a relative who had taken my father in temporarily. I was scalded because I had said yes to having sugar in a cup of tea. Saying that I would like sugar would have been a stressful event for my father and I recall him yelling at me, "What did you ask that for, you f – c - !" His choice of words was ugly.

On occasional days out, my father would often ruin them. Once, he threw the radio over a cliff and another time, my teddy bear was hurled over a cliff (what was it about cliffs?!) – the same teddy that he'd happily bought me 20 minutes earlier. Christmas was always hideous. My father would swear when he couldn't open a present that had too much tape on it or throw his Christmas dinner at the wall. My eldest sister now absolutely loves Christmas and cherishes every calm moment of it. I personally hate Christmas. It was never my father's intention to ruin special days, it was more that he was deeply damaged and traumatised, and simply 'living' was difficult for him. His bereavements had left him permanently unparented and emotionally broken. It was something that he never explored or worked through: it was not the 'done thing' in those days. He was often angry, self-loathing, quiet, ashamed or ill.

My father was damaged and my mother attempted to keep the peace so that my father wouldn't get angry and worst case, beat up my brother, Dave, who has learning disabilities. To this day, my two sisters and I, to a degree, parent our mother. I was the youngest of four children and I was the first, as an adult, to write to Social Services about my concerns. Such families tend to have a 'script' where they can be in complete denial about their own family situation. Both of my sisters are qualified nurses, one in mental health and the other caring for people with learning disabilities. Nursing is perhaps a way that people utilise their empathy and insight, in order to help others in need. Similarly, I was to follow a parallel career in social work management.

We were all victims as children, which I sensed as I put my head under my pillow, again and again, just hoping that the noise and 'buzzing' would go away. Night time was particularly difficult to sleep because of my father's behaviour. My neuro pathways were already being disturbed and this is how trauma imprints itself on the brain exceedingly early on.

As a child, I fainted a lot. Fainting was a default position to escape any stressful event. When children are placed in stressful situations, with no voice and no mental or physical escape, therapists say that fainting is the ultimate and final escape. Children will ask for help, call for help, self-soothe and look to a reliable adult or sibling. My neural pathways were already chaotic, so fainting became a coping mechanism. Fainting was also associated with trauma as the first thing most people do when someone faints is panic! I found it very disturbing to come round to the sound of sirens, lots of faces staring down at me and often, a distraught, frantic mother. I think I was the only person ever permanently excluded from my dentist surgery for fainting too often!

When I was four, I was knocked down and a car rolled over me. I was holding my sister's hand, on our way to buy chocolate from the local shop. I lost her grip, stepped out and the car went straight over me. I still remember the warmth as the car's undercarriage and engine burnt my skin. The driver, totally shocked (I still remember his face), carried me into my home. He told my mother that I was bleeding because I had wet myself and he felt the warmth of my urine. He calmly asked for an ambulance to be called. He was a kind man and I hope he learnt that I survived the incident. Due to my crippling shyness, it was two weeks before I confessed to the district nurse that I had a further burn on my bottom that I hadn't told anyone about! The look on her face was pure shock as she applied another dressing to add to the other burns.

I then had my own 'scud missile incident'. I choked on a gob stopper of that shape, which I'm sure children of the 1980's will remember. As I apparently turned blue, fortunately a friend whacked me on the back and the offending sweet flew out, so she pretty much saved my life. Even early on, I used humour as a way of coping. My daughter says to me now, "Mum, you are a responsible parent, the best ever, but you almost have a child humour outlook on the world." I think she's right!

The next significant memory I have is the yew tree incident. The yew tree was a mushroom-shaped tree with a hollow, spikey interior. I knew that tree like the back of my hand. Why, oh why, did I slip that day and impale myself on a sharp piece of the dagger-shaped wood? It was a wet day and I still remember sliding downwards, face to the tree. No-one was nearby so the only way to escape was to pull myself and part of the branch away with me. I hobbled into the kitchen and told my mother that my stomach ached. She said, "Never mind now." I told her that it really hurt, lifted my top up and showed her the large piece of wood sticking out of my abdomen. I was duly admitted to hospital for emergency surgery.

Due to my neurological composition, alcohol has never agreed with me. During my teenage years, I consumed a large amount of cider, which resulted in an out-of-body experience. I floated and recalled events that I just would not have otherwise known. These psychic happenings, or auras, have happened to me frequently, as they also do to one of my sisters, usually around death. My most significant vision was of my father coming to sit next to me shortly after he died. It's not something I really talk about; I try to put it down to a rational or logical explanation but there is often not one to be found. These happenings, I found out 20 years later, whilst on my Cruse training, are actually quite common with bereaved individuals.

Prior to starting secondary school, I was chronically and painfully shy. I wouldn't even answer if someone spoke to me, apart from my family, my teacher and my friend Kay. Kay is as chatty today as she was then and, in junior school, I welcomed how she would rescue me and talk on my behalf. I owe her a great debt. Kay also has happy memories of me being her first best friend when she joined our school, when the teacher cleverly gave me the role of being her buddy.

On commencing secondary school, I discovered that if I looked nice, giggled and engaged with people, then life could work better for me. I went from mute to giggly in six months. It was at this time that I also met Elaine, who is my best friend to this day. I can tell her anything and she will still laugh with me and love me unconditionally.

Around this time, I was rescued when I slipped through a frozen lake. It is often only when you look back that you realise you could have easily died. Yet I still remember that very deep sense of fear, as a raw emotion. Bereavements are not just about actual loss, they are intrinsically entwined in near-death experiences, relationships and trauma. Trauma bonds can also emerge when you love and rely on family members who may be suffering themselves. It's a negative form of bonding as it keeps you loyal to a destructive situation and you still feel reliant on that person, or people. The trick is not to be drawn into the same patterns later in life.

I am incredibly ashamed to say that my sister Pam and I were prolific teenage offenders, mainly thieving. We were 'caught' and accused of stealing from a chemist where we had not actually stolen anything ironically but we did have other stolen goods on us. I begged the manager not to call my parents and told him that my father would actually kill me. The manager took pity on us and let us go, which was the biggest relief of my life. I genuinely believe that my father would have killed any of us, if we had not moderated our behaviour.

Another significant event as a teenager was when the same sister, Kay and I were playing 'chicken' across the runway at Blackbushe Airport. I nearly got chopped up by a helicopter as I ducked underneath it, in motion. The airport came to a standstill and all aircraft were grounded. Apparently, a VIP had been waiting to land and we had caused an 'international incident'. I'm still not sure how it amounted to this at such a small airport but it was certainly a dangerous and reckless thing to do. I was genuinely remorseful and again, we were sent on our way with an extremely strict telling off.

At school, I was frequently in trouble, mainly for walking on the school roof, but I managed to charm my way out of trouble. I was smart and although I was naughty, my teachers seemed to like me. I returned to the school 20 years later, this time working as a youth justice officer. The deputy head recognised me, which I think must have made his day!

During my teenage years, I experienced two significant bereavements. My remaining grandparent (the only one who had not died before I was one) passed away suddenly of a heart attack. He was my Grandad Horace, who had a big, red strawberry nose, probably from drinking too much beer. But I liked that nose and I liked him. His garden was huge so we would walk around it for hours, talking and collecting huge buckets of runner beans and strawberries. I can still smell the strawberries as I think of his nose. He was a lovely man, always buying us a big bag of sweets every Saturday, which we would carefully share out into four portions when we got home. There was never an exact four of each item so you can imagine, with me being the youngest, how that went!

A short time later, my teenage school friend, Dean, died. The school provided scant information, other than to tell us that he had taken his own life. At our school reunion in 2000, everyone's school photographs were there except Dean's. He may have been erased from the school history, but his loss still lay heavy on our hearts. We remain an extraordinarily strong school year and support each other even now, through social media and meeting up.

Elaine still talks about the fear and anxiety of visiting my family home. She never told me at the time - perhaps she didn't properly reflect on her emotions - but she tells me now. The word 'resilience' has often been used to describe me and my two sisters. My brother is still living in the family home but my father has long since died. I will explore my next bereavements later in the book.

I had some great teachers but none of them referred us to Social Services, which is something that has always puzzled me. My brother has always had learning disabilities and went to a special school, but his behaviour was becoming more extreme. He would sometimes punch through doors or melodramatically wave bloodied knives around from meat preparation. On one occasion, a patient escaped from Broadmoor, a specialist, psychiatric hospital for the criminally insane, and the police turned up at our door: someone had reported concerning behaviour!

Whilst at secondary school, it was rather like being a member of the Mafia. If anyone upset me, my brother Dave, with his mad eyes and heavy build, would just lift them up and throw them over fences or walls. Dave's most dramatic episode was stealing a JCB digger! With the keys already in the ignition, he started driving around a building site. On arrival, the police officer waved and gestured for my brother to stop. Dave kept driving and the officer had to leap into a ditch to save his own life. That incident led my brother to the local magistrate's court. His psychologist's report described him as being an 'upstanding member of the community', who helped elderly neighbours with their gardening. The sad truth was that Dave carried out gardening tasks for them and then demanded money. He received a conditional discharge which was basically a form of punishment like a suspended sentence, reserved only for the least serious cases.

Whilst at Farnborough Sixth Form College, I had an extremely dramatic fainting episode in the middle of Farnborough town centre. This resulted in me experiencing another 10 strange faces looking down over me and hearing the familiar siren of an ambulance. I had a few other faints, mainly around alcohol consumption, which one male nurse interpreted as a seizure. I was referred to Neurology for further examination but was quickly discharged.

At 18 years of age, I moved out of the family home and shortly afterwards met a (later to be convicted) property fraudster. We lived together for 18 months and each day, people would arrive and stuff increasingly large amounts of money through our letter box. I'm talking bags and bags of money. We spent 18 months together but the seriousness of what I had witnessed only hit me eight years later when I received a bill for £44,000 for mortgage fraud. The investigation was eventually, much later, dropped against me. If I had been dishonest and pocketed even a small amount of that money, I would have been seriously rich by now. We lived a life of luxury - 'the high life' if you like - but at a young age, I learnt that money alone does not buy you happiness. I have bumped into this guy whilst out shopping a couple of times since, which has left my heart pounding so hard and fast that I could hardly breathe. It can be down to bad luck that some young adults find themselves in inappropriate relationships, which is why it's still important to 'look out for' your kids, even in their late teens and twenties.

———

When I walked out of that relationship, I had nowhere to go and I'd left with just a small rucksack of clothes. I didn't want him to suspect that I was leaving until I'd made my escape. I asked my mother if I could move back but she just couldn't cope with another person at home, due to the pressures from my brother and the fact that she could barely cope herself. I was homeless. If I had ever told my young offenders this, when I worked with them years later, they would have been shocked. One of them once asked me if I'd ever driven too fast on the motorway: I loved that they believed I would never have been in any kind of trouble!

After my move from luxury to homelessness in less than a day, my sister and I lived in a tent in Small Dole, near Brighton, for six months. Apart from the tent, our only other possessions were two motorbikes. We befriended the entire local population of wild animals (and I further enhanced my love of nature) and life was girlie and fun. We worked at nursing homes, mainly on the night shift, saving our hard-earned money until we were able to build up a deposit and rent a flat. Our other sister moved in too and we became known locally, in care home circles, as 'The Goddard Sisters'. My sister above me still recalls her time in Brighton as being the best summer of her life!

A couple of years later, we moved back to our home area of Surrey/Hampshire. One sister and I rented a house, with a mad lady and her evil cat. Around this time, I met my husband. Steve pretty much rescued me and also offered me somewhere decent to live. I will be forever grateful to him: it is at your lowest moments that you find out who is truly there for you. Meeting Steve not only made me feel happy and loved, it also enabled me to study, travel, get married and have children. Beyond the basic survival instinct, I was now actually living. And an added bonus during that time was that I was actually paid to go to university!

Concentrating on significant traumas and losses, I have had the misfortune of being present at two separate terrorist incidents. The first time, I was with my two sisters. We were sitting in a garden café in Cairo, enjoying afternoon tea, surrounded by an oasis of beautiful shrubs and flowers. You could not have created a more idyllic setting, as we enjoyed homemade cake and sipped tea. Next door, a terrorist incident took place at the Cairo Museum. The sounds and screams from the innocent victims haunt me today and I can still picture the surreal news coverage on CNN. Many years later, I was back in Egypt, with Steve, my sister Yonnie and her husband. We were staying on Isis Island on the River Nile, off Aswan. Again, we had to take cover when terrorists attacked Luxor and Aswan. The choice for some was either being hit by a bullet or the River Nile full of crocodiles. The sounds, again, still haunt me. Egypt has been one of the most beautiful countries I have visited but I will never return.

Steve came from a family of openness, the polar opposite to our more emotionally restrained family. He has a background of grammar school teaching and the Royal Military Police, Special Branch. His military mindset was quite different to anything I had experienced before but it was a welcome tonic to the chaos of my life. Steve's family seemed to drink alcohol more than ours and they were extremely frank and direct. Similar to boarding school culture, they had an approach to life that seemed centred around strategic survival personalities, where the parents are busy elsewhere. As adults, it is generally these people whose mantra is to think positive and work hard. I have come to quite like that sort of approach, for I embrace the optimism and positivity of it, but my critical brain pathways will never think that way: I am indeed wired differently.

I must mention here some further tragedies of school friends. My school year remains remarkably close even now, based partly upon shared bereavement trauma. There have been several natural deaths, including heart attacks, cancer and drug-induced sepsis but probably the most tragic was the murder of Julie Harrison and her daughter, Maisie. For those of you not familiar with the case, Julie and her young daughter were shot by Julie's ex-partner, in Aldershot, Hampshire. My best friend, Elaine, heard the news on the radio and will probably never forget that sensation of the world stopping in that moment. Julie and Elaine were also best friends during our school years; when Julie was 16 years old, she arrived at Elaine's house, needing urgent medical attention and Elaine needed to call an ambulance. She still has a recurring nightmare where she tries to dial 999 on an old-style telephone but her fingers will not work properly and she keeps mis-dialling, meaning she has to hang up and start again. Everyone, like Elaine, can feel ambivalence as to how much they can or should help others in crisis, without compromising their own need for 'mental space'.

Death of loved ones does certainly permeate through us like a ripple effect, bringing up different emotions for each individual. Emotions that have emerged relating to Julie's death include love, compassion, guilt, regret, depression and fear. We should all take comfort that we have often 'given' much more to those who have passed than we realised. Many of us on Facebook are often reminded of Julie and my heart continues to break for her and her little girl. There is nothing like social media to keep the past in the present, shifting the sands of time.

A few more years passed by and I reached my early thirties. My sister had had a child and I decided I really wanted one too. Steve and I had already been together for 10 years and we had travelled the world. I had spent seven years at university as I loved studying but when Steve said, "Are you ever going to get a job?!", I turned down a PhD. He'd made a valid point, although to be fair, I had been working part-time whilst studying, with the elderly and people with learning disabilities. Care work is a humbling yet fun job to undertake and I loved to hear the stories from some absolute characters.

Whilst studying for my first degree, a university friend of mine died. When the professors explained what had happened to her, they explained it in Latin. I gathered from her parents at the funeral that there was a problem with the brain and her body had become extremely swollen. We had a long conversation and they obviously took great comfort from talking about their daughter. Another bereavement and, as people know who have experienced multiple bereavements, each one comes with a memory of all those preceding it. By now, I was thinking that there must be something about me that attracts death but I now know that this is quite a common reaction for those who suffer multiple bereavements.

My first pregnancy was perhaps the worst of my bereavements and the hardest loss of my life. The level of pain is not a competition of grief, but something truly died inside me. I will never go back to the person I was before I miscarried twins. I've remained, in essence, shy again. In losing twins, I lost the potential future of what it would have been to have twins (although my two children of course made up for this loss). When my son went to school, his year group was considered 'special' because they had an extraordinary number of twins, which attracted a lot of media coverage. This was always a bittersweet reminder for me of what might have been. What was particularly helpful to me, as with any miscarriage, was the number of meaningful cards I received and not particularly the gifts or flowers.

Steve and I refer to the year I lost the twins as 'the bereavement year'. It was also the year that New York's Twin Towers were taken out by terrorists. Two of Steve's uncles died, we lost our beloved dog and both of our fathers died. My father died two months after I miscarried twins and I felt responsible on some level. He was due to have a heart operation on the Monday and was advised to come off his blood-thinning medication before being released for the weekend. Steve and I arrived before the ambulance and attempted to resuscitate him, without success. That is perhaps the worst memory I have 'buzzing' about in my 'neuro head'.

Less than a month later, the home telephone rang at 6am. I looked at Steve, fear in my eyes, and selfishly asked if he could take the call. Phone calls at 6am are never good news and he was told that his father had died. I felt deep guilt about not taking that call for him and still regret my impulsive decision. His father was a lovely human being who had been a father figure to me, representing what an 'ideal' father would be like. It was December and we hosted Christmas that year. It must have been quite miserable for those who attended!

It was not until a year later, after I had given birth to our son, Max, that I was referred to a clinical psychologist for bereavement therapy because I kept going cross-eyed and experiencing 'twinning', where I imagined I was seeing two of everything. The therapist told me that it would have been impossible to resuscitate my father because a heart attack of that sudden nature would have required medical equipment such as a defibrillator. It was quite healing to learn that nothing I could have done at the time would have changed the outcome. I was also experiencing delayed grief, as during my pregnancy, I had been told by many well-meaning friends 'not to grieve as it may harm the baby'. I was pregnant two months after 'the bereavement year'.

When Max was born, he was not breathing. He was resuscitated and placed in the Special Care Baby Unit (SCBU), after turning blue. The amazing staff at the hospital saved his life. He is bright as a button now and you would not believe he had such a touch and go start. For anyone who has not been to SCBU, it is a deeply haunting and humbling place to visit. Many of the babies have been born prematurely (Max was late, with low sugar and low temperature) and when they are born very early, they look almost transparent. It is a life-changing, horrific and surreal experience, also observing other parents and seeing in their eyes that their baby is not necessarily going to make it.

Between losing twins, giving birth to Max and conceiving my daughter, Ruby-Rose, I had many miscarriages. I am ashamed to say I do not know how many, as sometimes I would get a positive pregnancy test, only to bleed within two weeks. I would estimate that I had in excess of 15 miscarriages. My then GP finally referred me to a specialist after three 'recognised' miscarriages. For me, every loss was a lost future. Driven almost to madness, if someone had put a gun in my hand during that time, I'm not sure I would trust myself, such is the pain of multiple miscarriage. The emotional pain of loss and trauma really can drive people to murder and I totally get that. My lucid dreams got worse and I even 'killed' people in my dreams. Interestingly, days before my twin miscarriage, I dreamt of a young girl playing on a swing and then I lost her from view. I remember the dream vividly to this day. The little girl was Ruby-Rose, my daughter, although the dream was many years before she was born. Her appearance was so distinct, she was that girl, waiting in the wings of life.

Since then, we lost more dear school friends, which was bizarrely becoming the norm. During a visit to the infertility gynaecologist, I had a laparoscopy, which revealed a large 'chocolate cyst'. I was given antibiotics to decrease my inflammation. I was very sick but miraculously, I conceived my daughter. It was even more surprising as Steve was bedbound after a serious motorbike accident. Ruby-Rose was seven years in the making but like Max, she was well worth the wait. The midwife who delivered her was an amazing human being and I believe that midwives are often the therapeutic antidote to death.

You cannot underestimate the trauma and loss of miscarriage. In attempting to conceive, sex becomes a military operation, planned to the letter for perfect timing. If you want to ruin a marriage and/or sex life, look no further than couples contemplating, executing and living through the trauma of parental loss and hope. Julia Bueno states, "Recurrent miscarriage is a reproductive experience of its own, a deeply unpleasant order. When I think of any stories I know about, couples enduring this private hell, I am reminded of both our potentially consuming and agonising desire to conceive and the indefatigable resilience of the human spirit."

A few years later, Steve's mother and great aunt died, which were both quite a shock to me. I took the call about his mother's death and we were the last relatives to see his great aunt alive. When I took the call from my mother-in-law's neighbour, I actually felt quite faint; and whilst we sat with his great aunt, she was asking where all the other relatives were. By this time, we were becoming quite proficient at arranging funerals! Around this time, my friend Diane also passed away. She was sent for a CT scan but it was too late and she was gone two weeks later. When my friend Juana called to tell me the news, I said, "It's Diane, isn't it". I don't know what made me say that, as the last I knew, she thought that she had ME. A couple more of my school friends also died, then more recently, a friend of the family, Wilko, lost his battle with face cancer.

It was around this time that my neurological symptoms started: my brain could take no more. Including my miscarriages, I would estimate that I have experienced more than 40 bereavements and this does not include every bereavement, just the most painful and traumatic ones. If I were explaining myself to someone in just five words, 'bereaved' would be up there.

I was recently chatting to my daughter about my 25 bereavements (excluding the miscarriages, due to her young age). I was saying how, since Covid-19, my bereavements did not seem so huge anymore and the experience had put everything into perspective. She laughed and said, quite maturely, "Mum, it's taken 55,000 deaths to heal you." I apologised to her as it sounded so disrespectful and self-centred, with all those lives tragically lost but, if I am honest, yes, that was the only thing that put my losses into any shared social perspective. I no longer felt I was carrying the 'bereavement banner' over my head.

During the Covid-19 pandemic, I undertook some online therapy, which was excellent. Out of healing came light and, on that day, I phoned up and volunteered for 'Cruse Bereavement Care', which provides a free listening helpline and bereavement counselling to people suffering from grief. The training to become a volunteer is excellent and I personally found it so helpful on an emotional level. I felt I had unpicked my own grief enough and was in a good position to positively help others.

*"Vulnerability is terrifying.
The courage it takes to reveal
your heart is one of the most
daunting, and yet rewarding
experiences in life.
It will set you free."*

The Better Man Project

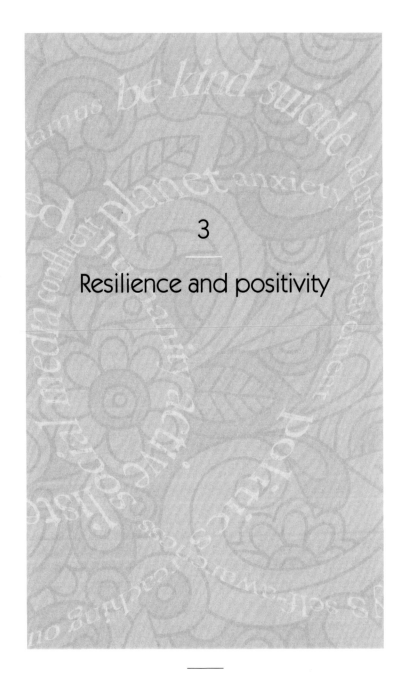

3

Resilience and positivity

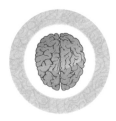

You may not believe it but I am naturally a very positive, insightful and optimistic person, and a great friend. If you have my friendship, you have it for life. But where does this resilience and positivity come from?

The main positive memories I have of my childhood are of our beloved garden and trips to many National Trust establishments. My parents' knowledge of gardening was impressive. It clearly was the thing that calmed and nourished them both. My parents were two incredibly intelligent human beings. My father would generally answer 80% of the questions on the general knowledge part of Mastermind. He was well read, especially given that he had been pulled from pillar to post due to his childhood losses, sometimes sharing a bed due to lack of space. When he lost his mother, he didn't live with his father.

Gardening was definitely my parents' passion and their 'happy place'. The quote by Jenny Uglow always resonates with me: "We may think we are nurturing our garden, but of course it's our garden that is really nurturing us." There is something very healing about nature and I appreciate it every waking moment. I do believe that the beauty of nature provides calmness and resilience. I am also drawn to the ocean. The rhythm of nature is strangely calming and meditative. The colours, the textures, the nurturing… and rather like the power of dogs, they give back, they do not argue, they are truly unconditional.

My friends will tell you that humour and charm is what has made me resilient. I was always able to make friends and keep friends, something that my parents struggled to do. They would often fall out with relatives and employers, regressing back to their childhood 'positions' of pushing people away. My mother had been an only child and my father ended up emotionally alone, despite having the two sisters (early on) and one very socially awkward brother, who died, alone, shortly after he did.

I think significant figures, apart from my grandad, were in short supply up to the age of 11. One area that I always excelled in was sport, even in junior school, and sport is an area where growth and self-esteem can be built. It was perhaps through sport that I learnt about ethics and being part of a team. The individual exception was my friend Kay, at junior school, who emotionally contained me and even answered for me. Kay is still a remarkable human being, with extraordinarily strong magnetic fields. I owe her a lot. In secondary school, I had some great friends and Elaine is still my best friend. She will tell you that we hated each other when we first met, but for me, that was never the case. She was feisty and outspoken, and she has been my greatest role model.

At secondary school, the teachers liked me, or were at least amused by me, no-one more so than my maths teacher, Mr Harris. He knew I was brighter than I looked and laughed when I completed my maths questions in top speed so I could go on to distract those around me. Matt, my first proper boyfriend, was highly intelligent and gave me the confidence to 'move' in any circle I chose. As a result, I was a girl who could hang out with anyone, if they were good people. It held me in good stead for making report representations to judges, in the Crown Court.

I studied Hair and Beauty at college, as all my friends were undertaking the same course: that was my motivation. It is a shallow industry, which I never went into, but I do still use these skills in my spare time. At college, I started getting A grades and distinctions. By this time, I knew I was quite bright. Intelligence provides resilience in itself, as it means you can use your brain and take up opportunities to better yourself. Later, in youth justice, the judges always wanted to hear the views of the young, pretty youth justice officer in front of them, despite already having a well-prepared pre-sentence report. They always seemed to have a little chuckle and went along with my proposals!

Prior to university, I undertook an access course to science and humanities, which was equivalent to A-levels. The course tutor and the maths teacher were major role models for me. At university, during three courses, I met many inspiring people who I hold in great affection. Studying social work for my Masters and learning counselling and active listening skills undoubtedly taught me some great practical skills. Mark Neal and Peter Pettit stand out. Peter would say, "You're as bright as a button, Wendy." He always warmed my heart, in a paternal kind of way.

I am lucky to have many good friends and a number of them would come to my aid if I called on them in the early hours. Like flowers, I nurture my friends and many of my good friendships have been long-lasting. Do not always look to expand your network, always cherish the good ones you have. I have also always undertaken a lot of training and development, so I am a good manager of people and my work relationships, overall, have been positive. I could name a couple of 'toxic' line managers I've had but taking the positives out of it, they at least have taught me how not to manage people! I have found it is best to avoid shallow, pretentious and vain people who inadvertently drain the hell out of you. I feel blessed, as a human being, to have approximately 10 very good friends in my life.

So far, I've told you a bit about me so you can start to see that we have to be understanding of people as we just do not know where anyone has 'walked' to get to where they are today. So, the first part of bereavement support, 'being kind' and 'heads together' is about actively listening to people's life trajectories and not judging them. This is the foundation of a tolerant and understanding society. It is also relevant to the world stage and the loss of the planet and its inhabitants.

_____

"To plant a garden is to believe in tomorrow."

Audrey Hepburn

_____

4

Health news

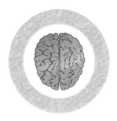

I believe that often, but not always, poor mental health and physical ill health mirror one another, or at least have an impact on each other. Poor health is draining. Alongside this is the way in which people treat you along the journey. I'd had, up to now, good experiences in maternity, general practice and gynae.

Bereavement had always been a constant cause of stress within my head and in December 2015, I started to experience abdominal pains. Due to my previous gynaecological issues, I automatically assumed that this was the problem again. I was given a smear test that came back abnormal. At this point, I still had the abdominal pains and was convinced that I was dying. During this stressful time, my mother-in-law passed away. It was the meeting of too many emotional strains, which I think of now as an emotional thunderstorm.

At this time, I declared to my former GP, "I don't know what is wrong but I think I'm dying." I had developed electric misfiring running down my arms and legs. My feet were hot. I had altered sensations and was, on the inside, hysterical and frightened. I believe, to this day, that at that time, I should have been admitted into hospital. Something felt seriously wrong. One thing was for sure, I needed more than just paracetamol and being told not to worry.

The biopsy of my cervix came back negative but the new, peripheral neuropathy (altered sensation to hands and feet) in its various guises, remained. It is still very much with me to this day. A referral was made to a neurology specialist and the wait began.

That spring and summer, I recall various events, such as trips to the funfair and being on holiday, yet struggling with steps and thinking, "Oh my, this is not right." It was indeed a sequence of mini traumas, such as going out with my friends, and inside I felt I was dying. I continued to have 'electric' misfiring rushing through my body. The wait for a neurological appointment seemed endless – all I wanted was tests and answers!

Neurology is the poor cousin to cancer and heart disease, I conceded at the time. If you have never waited in a neurology waiting room, then consider yourself lucky. Of course, there are 'strong' people in these clinics, but my snapshot experience was of a vulnerable group who did not seem to have a very strong voice, compared to those advocating cancer care. There remains a certain anxiety and nervousness around anything to do with the brain. I kept my health journey quiet from many school mums, fearing that they would not let their children play with mine. My experience is that when you do open up, some individuals walk away and keep their distance, yet some stay. It is without doubt that neurological treatment can leave patients feeling isolated and leave friends and relatives at a loss as to what to say. It is at these times that you find out who your true friends are. The revelation can be surprising, so do not be quick to give up on people and never be too hasty to judge someone else's health issue.

I eventually had a nerve conductor test in December 2016 and a head MRI in January 2017, both of which came back negative. The MRI was terrifying. I was put into an old-fashioned tube and I felt claustrophobic, which is a common fear for trauma children as they feel they have no form of escape. I felt an immense and overwhelming sense of fear and anxiety. My husband was with me for support and also two male technicians, all of whom were over six feet tall. In the spirit of humour, the memory of being consoled by three strapping men still makes me chuckle even now when I recall it. Humour is perhaps the greatest device in our life toolbox.

The same symptoms developed and work, as a fostering manager, continued to be stressful, with further threats of job cuts. After putting in years of hard work, the entire industry was being 'audited' and appraised by a minority of aggressive women. These particular women were not good in times of crisis themselves but were happy to rip the guts out of other people's lives. The only consolation was that I was not destitute but for some, it was seriously affecting their health and livelihood. This is not to say that public services should not be reviewed but there is a more humane way of doing so. The job cuts that I have witnessed have often been poorly managed and devastating to individuals and their families.

Many months later, I was told, not in any formal sense, that my job was safe after all. They were looking qualitatively rather than quantitively: this was meant to make me feel better and valued! No real explanations, no apology. Carefully considered job cuts do have to be made sometimes, however we should all treat other human beings with compassion and care.

That year saw numerous visits back to my former GP as I wanted further tests. In my view, I could have been referred for repeat nerve conductor studies, MRIs of my hands and feet, lumber samples, plasma exchange and antibiotics. After some persistence, she did refer me back to the hospital but by this time, she was repeatedly writing on my medical notes, "Wendy just needs to stop worrying." She was trying to reassure me by saying I should not worry but I felt it was quite rational and normal to worry about my symptoms. I felt out of control because my symptoms were unnerving and unsettling; I couldn't help but worry. I think she was, sincerely, just trying to help me.

In December 2017, I turned up to the Neurology department,

still with twitches, weakness and altered sensation. I was optimistic as I had voiced my concerns on several occasions about waiting times. The Care Commission and my MP were now involved: surely now they would give me another nerve conductor test, at the very least, as these results can change over time.

I arrived for my appointment, refreshed from some recent sunshine abroad, feeling hopeful. There is nothing worse than having your expectations dashed. My husband came with me, having been briefed on which of my symptoms to concentrate on. In front of me was a prominent neurologist and two spotty medical students. The neurologist took me by the hand (seriously, it's quite funny to recall it now) and explained that he had read my notes and was not offering anything further. The students shuffled nervously. One looked like a combination of Ed Sheeran and Colin Baker with curly reddish-brown hair and the other just sat there looking incredibly awkward, with all the hand-holding going on!

Emotionally, the words went over my head and I sensed, rather than heard, my husband talking about my sleep problems (and, in my view, going majorly off track about my symptoms). I was in this room with four strapping men - more men. I have nothing against men. They are often so funny but at this moment, I wanted to scream. I felt that bizarre mixture of stereotypical reassurance because I was dealing with medical professionals, yet on the other hand, also a sense of unease that my symptoms had gone unheard. I did not have the medical knowledge to challenge them, apart from to ask for more nerve tests and explain my symptoms again. The neurologist said that would not be possible and continued to hold my hand. He meant well and he had kind eyes but my voice and symptoms had not been heard. They were all having a jolly old chatter about the army days whilst I was sitting there, feeling pretty devastated if I'm honest.

The receptionist asked if I would like to fill in a feedback card and (quite rudely, I'm ashamed to say, as she was actually quite nice) I told her exactly what she could do with her feedback cards. At least I was in the Neurology department, where they seem to expect you to be a little mad! I raged at my husband down the hospital corridors, with extraordinarily little discretion. I completely lost my usual sense of composure and I was seething.

My symptoms continued. From the top of my head down to my toes, they were there to remind me that my life was not so perfect. More symptoms emerged: a buzzing head, altered tongue, shooting pains in my jaw, arm ache, weak, stiff and twitching hands, pounding heart, changed appearance to skin and weak ankles. Some of these symptoms were worse than they are now.

Another locum GP referred me to a specialist in London, who sent the referral back to a different local hospital. I would have to wait until August 2018.

I decided to go privately which proved to be a waste of money. I saw a female neurologist….I was so hopeful! Her name suggested, with my strange sense of stereotyping, that she might be reasonably young. I hoped that maybe she would be able to understand and empathise with my physical and emotional symptoms, but no. She just went on the 'signs'. I could physically walk across the room so she deduced that I must be okay. She diagnosed me with 'ill health anxiety'. I was beyond exasperated. Being worried about symptoms is not the same as ill health anxiety. I would have to wait a further few months for more tests.

A diagnosis of ill health anxiety is difficult. In my view, this centres around what is said and what is heard. The neurologist probably felt that, following a long discussion with me, I'd become overly focused upon my symptoms. Again, I think her intention was to reassure me. What I was hearing, on a purely emotional level, was that everyone had died around me and the same could happen to me. On reflection, I can see why people are diagnosed with such terms. However, I went in expecting a clear diagnosis and an ongoing plan. I still do not feel that I have ill health anxiety but

I do believe chronic symptoms can be an outcome of our genes, our traumas and our life course. This can shift the challenges for an individual to a more sociological and psychological level. Perhaps at this stage, it might be useful to see a psychologist or wellbeing coach, in tandem with having a neurological discussion or examination.

I found a very competent acupuncturist, who was emotionally sound and had a great sense of humour, so he was more than able to take my life story of bereavement and loss. He was the first person I had explained my entire life story to, poor guy, and we were actually in hysterics by the end of it! Furthermore, his explanations were holistic, insightful, well explained and helpful. He taught me about my thyroid, cells, enzymes and lots of other medical stuff. He had, in the past, been a pharmacist, but had retrained. He was sceptical of the medical industry, medicines and how some of them did not work. He was pretty cynical about his past experiences and we used to rage at the world. During that time, I was still feeling angry myself, so he came along at a good time.

My former GP meanwhile was suggesting Piriton for the tongue tingling. I rescheduled another appointment and saw one of the locums, who I'd seen before. For the same lip and tongue symptoms, he said that it was likely to be neurological. If other tests were coming back 'clean,' he suggested that I ask for my neurology appointment to be brought forward. It is so important to have your symptoms validated.

I saw my then GP one more time who told me to embrace my symptoms and be 'joyful'. I asked her if she could refer me for a private MRI (which I would pay for) but she refused.

I saw the neurology specialist again who stated that I had 'trust issues and a mistrust of authority'. I objected to this comment because I couldn't see how, under any circumstances, it could be deemed helpful. I think the reason I took such exception to the neurologist's comment was because it triggered emotions in me surrounding my father's passing. He died on an NHS London waiting list, whilst being sent home for the weekend and told to come off his warfarin. I tried to resuscitate him and I was the one who had to explain to my mother and siblings that he had died. Therefore, being told that I had trust issues was really painful – it didn't mean I had a mistrust of professionals in general. Now, on reflection, I believe I probably overreacted due to my raw emotions at that time. I did actually write to apologise to my neurologist. Clearly, he didn't know my life course and I had been a bit dramatic. Issues of transference can arise when 'red flags' are triggered.

Meanwhile at work, my line manager, OH and HR had been really understanding. Six months after my neurology appointment, my promised nerve conductor studies referral had still not been sought. I wrote to the Chief Executive and the appointment was quickly arranged but then deferred due to Covid-19.

Coming back to 2019, I had to choose my new GP. I chose Dr X. I'd met him before and he was direct and straight to the point. This was a good move. He has been very understanding and I would say that he has almost taken my bereavement anger away. That is some enormous achievement. He is one of those people who doesn't realise just how funny he is. He walked my journey with me and understood me, saying that I am 'an ongoing investigation!' Medicine was definitely a vocation for him; my appointments with him always went over…10 minutes was never enough time. The great sadness of Covid-19 was that this relationship would inevitably be halted. On moving between Hampshire and Cornwall, he was one of a small group of people I really missed. I respected him a lot as a human being.

I had some news from my January 2020 MRI: I found out that I have a 'cavernoma'. I received this news from my neurologist in the post. Lockdown had not yet begun when I received it. It did not state where the cavernoma was located and I was left worried for weeks, having nightmares about it being located on my brain stem.

Cavernomas are a rare disease affecting the brain, spine or body. They are a cluster of abnormal blood vessels and are sometimes known as cavernous angiomas, cavernous haemangiomas or cerebral cavernous malformations (CCM). A typical cavernoma looks like a raspberry in appearance. Cavernomas come under the definition of being a benign tumour and are most typically located within the brain. They are frequently described as incidental (randomly appearing) or inherited. In the case of inherited cavernomas, there is a gene that predisposes some individuals to have them, often, but not always, in multiple frequency. Rather like what is beginning to be described as 'long Covid', we find here a middle ground. There is a big unrecognised space between an inactive and a bleeding cavernoma. The comparison is purely my own interpretation, based upon symptoms that are up for debate, on their causation. Many people I have spoken to or liaised with, who have cavernomas, believe that their 'inactive' or mildly acting cavernoma plays havoc on their bodily/nervous system.

There are many people who are told by professionals that their cavernoma (or cavernomas) has no effect and no correlation with other symptoms in their body, despite its location in the brain. These altered sensations, feelings of pain and emotional intrusions, can sometimes have a profound effect on one's quality of life. Where a correlation or definitive diagnosis is made, it can be positive in validating the presence and impact of such symptoms. Rather like 'labelling,' it is also important to not label unnecessarily; but for some, this can provide an explanation to an individual's behaviour and how they interact within their social support network.

My 6mm cavernoma is located in my right parietal lobe and I have communicated with many individuals who have a similarly located inactive cavernoma and who are experiencing almost identical symptoms to my own. Rather like disorders such as ME and fibromyalgia, symptoms are often obscure and do not always lend themselves to a written vocabulary. Some symptoms have to be experienced to be understood and it is important for friends and family to listen carefully. Symptoms from cavernomas can range from tingling, tinnitus, altered sensation, other worldliness, dizziness, seizures, migraines, anxiety, unusual temperature control, head pulsating, weakness and/or altered senses. However, everyone is so different: many people may have no symptoms at all yet for others, it can be potentially life-threatening, Cavernomas on the brain stem are often a cause for concern but can also be 'inactive'. Other cavernomas can be placed in clear or obscure parts of the brain. As medical, diagnostic and treatment skills improve, more cavernomas are being located, monitored and/or treated.

My symptoms are formally diagnosed as a functional neurological disorder (FND), however it is my personal view that my cavernoma causes some of my neurological symptoms. We are all wired differently and I am particularly prone to fainting, feeling faint on aeroplanes (sorry to the individuals and staff who have flown with me, especially on the occasion that I ruined a stranger's first-class experience!), electric misfiring, headaches, buzzing, tinnitus, ears ringing, altered sensation/neuropathy in my hands and feet, with no diagnosis of diabetes or B12 deficiency, word muddling and brain fog. My father had a diagnosis of Myasthenia gravis, which is perhaps why I may have a propensity to adverse neurological occurrences.

Such symptoms are not currently prioritised by the NHS for early appointments but clearly, early intervention can potentially help save costs further down the line. The same could be said regarding the mental wellbeing of patients, regarding trauma, bereavement and/or chronic illness of all age groups. Sometimes specialist intervention is required, so that a holistic, confluent and/ or psychodynamic transformation can begin to occur.

The presence of cavernomas has recently become more widely recognised by the general public, as they have been used in storylines, on mainstream television and other purchased channels. This serves to demystify a disorder which is sometimes, but not always, a hidden illness. The challenge to the neurologist is to be entirely sensitive to the life course and the holistic workings of the mind and body. The brain and individuals are indeed both complex and complicated.

Around this time, all neurology appointments were put on hold due to Covid-19. My GP phoned and explained my cavernoma to me, which I appreciated. It is 6mm in length and is in my right parietal lobe. I am a member of the 'Cavernoma Alliance UK' and they are of the opinion that my symptoms are a result of the cavernoma. The Chief Executive and Service Manager are also promising to expedite my tests when Covid-19 makes it safe to do so. I have appreciated their intervention during what has been a very busy and stressful time for the NHS.

There is the big issue of missed diagnoses. There is a lot of literature about patients who have had neurological symptoms but a diagnosis has been missed or delayed. This is often because it's too early to show up on a nerve conductor test, or patients are discharged with a conversation, rather than more exploratory tests. For many people, with various illnesses and disorders, their illness is 'invisible'.

A lot of emphasis is based upon everything being caused by stress: stress plays a part but its role can often be exaggerated. I am a positive person but I got sick. This can happen to anyone. The best advice I can give is to stand by a friend or relative who may be struggling with health, mental or emotional issues and provide genuine, unconditional support.

_____

"Let it hurt. Let it bleed.
Let it heal. And let it go."

Nikita Gill

_____

5

My thoughts and
interpretations

I find the topic of lucid dreaming interesting. When I started to get sick, I was sleeping very badly and my husband was leaving to go to work incredibly early in the morning. At the time of night when my body should have been replenishing itself, mine was struggling. During my earlier adult life, I would regularly wake up in the middle of the night and be 'shivering' but not cold. I would be unable to stop myself shaking and would just breathe slowly and carefully for about ten minutes and wait for the feeling to pass. This went on for a couple of decades.

Having carried out a huge amount of research, my personal opinion is that ALS (amyotrophic lateral sclerosis) and MND (motor neurone disease) doctors are barking up the wrong tree! They look at proteins, DNA and gut analysis, seeing how the body changes, but they are looking at outcomes, in my view. They need to look earlier in the course of disease, combined with DNA factors. I believe that the body and mind are connected and this is generally recognised. When I got sick, I could feel the neurones or 'electrics' misfiring from the brain down my arms and legs. I do not have an ALS diagnosis as I am still being investigated, but my neurologists have consistently ruled out this diagnosis.

After I'd had an abnormal smear test and was waiting for the results, I was convinced I was dying. Do soldiers sometimes have the same fear? They might have an anxiety brought on by the fear of death, so does the body, misunderstanding the signals, go into overdrive? Then add poor sleep and lucid dreaming into the mix. When I lucid dream, I do not always control what happens but I do, to a degree. I am in the dreams, experiencing them and can be killing someone or going down a swim shute! Being a lucid dreamer means that you actually 'live' the experience. I am sure, for those of us that regularly dream like this, it must be difficult for the body to achieve deep, restorative sleep.

Since the Coronavirus crisis, my lucid dreaming has become much more frequent. These dreams disturb me greatly and I am not yet at a place where I can record them here in detail. Out of everything in life, they spook me out the most.

My muscles tense when I am sleeping, which I believe contributes to degeneration and also poor mental health. I have not always coped very well with extremes. I fainted a lot as a child and have always easily lost consciousness. My brain is overly sensitive and, as an adult, I have learnt relaxation techniques to avoid passing out. I believe that neurological happenings can sometimes have a lot to do with an unsettled mind and body.

Shortly after Ruby-Rose was born, I had the swine flu vaccination. From then on, my symptoms gradually emerged. There has been significant research carried out concerning the link between the swine flu vaccination and Guillain-Barre syndrome, which has some similarities to my early symptoms. My personal view though remains that vaccinations have been for the greater good, regarding world health. During that time, I was also overdosing on vitamin pills in the belief that they would help me. I now believe that they did more harm than good.

100 trillion organisms live in our guts and they comprise 90% of the cells of our bodies. They contain bacteria, archaea, eukaryotic parasites, protozoan and fungi. Deans (2004) talks about the brain/gut connection:

"What do they have to do with psychiatry? It turns out way more than we might have suspected. The gut and brain have a steady ability to communicate via the nervous system, hormones, and the immune system. Some of the microbiome can release neurotransmitters, just like our own neurons do, speaking to the brain in its own language via the vagus nerve."

The body responds to both mental and physical stress via the hypothalamic-pituitary-adrenal axis, known as your 'fight or flight' system. Deans reflects that as your head pounds, your pupils dilate, your hair stands on end, natural steroids and adrenaline flood your system to strengthen your muscles and give you an extra burst of speed. Even your platelets change shape, becoming stickier, leaving you less likely to bleed out if you are attacked. Under conditions of ongoing mental or physical overload however, the signals become distorted, leading to symptoms of chronic stress. This includes mental issues such as anxiety or clinical depression, but also physical problems such as chronic gut problems, headaches and high blood pressure.

The second underlying system, the immune system, is far more complex and works at a cellular level. The immune system works effectively and inflammation sometimes assists on a positive level. However, chronic levels of inflammatory response can also lead to all sorts of chronic disease, for example, depression, high blood pressure, neurological disease and cancer.

Gut bacteria can interact with the immune system to cause the release of inflammatory cytokines, stress steroids and a systemic stress response. Gut bacteria can have a positive or negative impact on the body and is closely related to poverty, mental wellbeing and disrupted support systems. Interestingly, new research has also found a link between cavernomas and poor gut health.

Bad gut health can affect certain neurotransmitter receptors, which are important in the regulation of mood, anxiety and closely related to psychosis, schizophrenia and bipolar disorder. There is also evidence that stress can affect the microbiome, which again is exacerbated by poor mental health and/or poverty.

The use of an acupuncturist can help to understand how hormones, enzymes and cells work but this treatment is not generally available on the NHS. How many people realise that we need fat in our bodies for cellular health? The low-fat diet was a mis-sold reality, in my opinion, which has increased sugar calories into thousands of people, often with negative consequences. I think it's important for the bereaved to try and eat a healthy, nutritionally-balanced diet. This can help with routine, mood, self-esteem, motivation, focus and social interaction.

My theory is that neurologists are currently looking at genes, proteins and lifestyle and how the body presents on results using a 'medical model'. The reality is that every part of the body is inter-connected. It would be good to hopefully see a more multi-agency, holistic approach to neurological health and wellbeing. The psychological undercurrents of FND and similar disorders could be explored in a creative way, through therapies such as group reflection and EMDR (Eye Movement Desensitisation and Reprocessing). This is a psychotherapy that enables people to heal from the symptoms and emotional distress that are the result of disturbing life experiences.

The following are some of the things that I am sensitive to, which seem to have an impact on my brain:

- Trauma
- Bereavement
- Hydrogen peroxide on skin
- Bleach in cleaning products
- Most hair dyes
- Tea tree oil
- Fake nails/procedures
- Diet pills
- Fake tan
- Biopsies on cervix
- Deep root canal treatment

I could feel pings in my body during these procedures. These are everyday items/activities that can be 'toxic' without people realising.

I have just finished reading a book called 'Lost Connections' by Johann Hari. It was an interesting read, basically stating that some anti-depression pills do not work. The scientists know that they frequently don't work long-term but it can sometimes be about the drugs companies making money. Hari points to happiness being found through better social connections and having a greater sense of love and belonging. Using anti-depressants for some individuals is essential but should only be prescribed when they are 100% required.

When someone tells you to stop worrying in a hundred different ways, they are suggesting that if you stop worrying, you will get better. This is not true: cancer does not just go away on its own and nor do many other conditions.

I had noticed in the years leading up to my symptoms starting that a kind of electric malfunction would occur. Please note though, I have always been different, sensitive and a frequent fainter. As I have stated, tea tree oil when washing my hair or body, root canal treatment, use of hair dye and nail varnish remover would all create an 'electric ping' in my brain which ceased after I stopped using these substances. I would also get this 'ping' when having gel nail treatments, from the ultraviolet light. We have learnt, over time, that natural tends to be best, generally speaking. I therefore wonder if it may be useful to look to electrics/robotics/mechanical engineers/scientists for answers?

I have not slept well for 18 years, since becoming a parent and I think this seems to have had an impact on my health. Research has shown that there is a higher propensity to neurological disorders within military personnel. When deployed on active duty, army recruits can also experience the 'jump impact' when asleep that I previously described, on the body's 'electrics'. You sleep when you can, in an often haphazard pattern, often needing to remain hyper alert and vigilant. There is also an issue of noise impacting on the sleeping body.

I am not from an army background but my husband served in the military police, so I have some insight into the sleeping patterns and mentality of this cohort. Incidentally, I always wake 3.5 hours into sleep, which is common too with those witnessing 'army trauma'. Can illness develop if you do not reach a state of 'deep sleep'? Are all illnesses, including neurological issues, mental illness and cancer, potentially caused where the body does not have chance to recover each day and is pushed to the limit? We can now easily and quite cheaply use watch-type devices such as Fitbits, to gauge the quality of our sleep. I have on average 50 minutes of 'deep sleep' each night, compared to my husband, who gets several hours! There is plenty of evidence to suggest that lack of sleep has multiple negative impacts on both the mind and body.

I think a lack of water may also impact on the body as I used to drink copious amounts of slim-line cola, believing this to be 'low fat,' until I realised it had a potentially harmful effect. Dehydration is another regular occurrence upon serving military personnel. For around a year prior to my symptoms appearing significantly, I used a fat-reducing diet tablet after every meal (the brand has now been taken off the market), which definitely had a negative impact on my body. Taking fat out of your diet completely and using diet soda drinks produces a 'perfect storm' to potentially wreck your immune system. Additionally, low vitamin D, which is common in the UK, prevents effective processing in the body. Both neurotrophic factors and negative protein alterations, which can be caused by lack of vitamin D, have been implicated in several neuromuscular and neurological diseases, including ALS, functional neurological disorders and multiple sclerosis.

---

5 | My thoughts and interpretations

———————

*"I know now that we never get over great losses;
we absorb them and they carve us into different, often kinder creatures."*

Cruse Bereavement Care

———————

6

The theories behind
bereavement and loss

To better understand ourselves and others, let's start with the link between our 'inner child' and our adult selves. This is in order to recall where we fit in and where others fit in. It is easy to then relate this to the 'adult wound' and our adult 'personality' traits. It explains why we act differently around different people and how we can all easily regress, following a loss, particularly whilst under stress, to our default positions.

Lindenfield (2000) outlines the following useful chart:

Sabotage	Words or thoughts	Inner child wound
Over-compensation	"I'm going to make sure my children don't have to go through what I went through."	Often the result of hurt or disappointment.
Over-dependency	"I'm sure I'm doing it wrong, I'll have to ask Jill or get a new book on the subject."	Often a result of not having enough approval.
Inappropriate imitation	"We always did it this way when I was a child."	Often the result of love being given too conditionally.
Over-protectiveness	"A person can't be too careful."	Often the result of insecurity, frightening experiences or being 'smothered' with protection.
Over-ambitiousness	"Only 'A' grades are good enough."	Often a result of having under-achieved as a child.
Perfectionism	"There's no point in trying if I can't do it properly."	Often the result of not being allowed to make mistakes or take risks.

Sabotage	Words or thoughts	Inner child wound
Over-seriousness	"Life is hard – the sooner my children learn that lesson the better."	Often the result of having had to grow up too quickly.
Irresponsibility	"Let's have another drink and let fate take care of it tomorrow."	Often the result of being either over or under-controlled as a child.
Revenge	"It won't do them any harm to suffer a bit – we had it a lot tougher than them."	Often the result of emotional or physical abuse.
Bullying	"You'll do as I say or else."	Often a result of having been hurt and deprived of reasonable rights as a child.
Inflexibility	"You've made your bed, now you have to lie in it."	Often a result of having to come to terms with apparently unchangeable negative situations.
Uncontrolled emotions	"I couldn't stop myself, you made me so angry."	Often a result of having emotions repressed and not being given advice on how to handle them.

Most adults, at some point, will consciously or unconsciously push people away because of the fear of getting hurt or being rejected. Each individual can gain a greater insight into themselves if they are honest about the patterns they tend to follow with others. Once a higher level of insight is achieved, you can be 'free' to be yourself and act in a transpersonal and transparent way.

By this, I mean you can achieve a higher level of yourself, insightful but free of the past and able to enjoy the very moment you are in. This enables people to seek out 'good' relationships which make them feel valued and loved. This applies to intimate, platonic or business relationships.

We should strive to be honest, warm, welcoming and accepting as these traits usually also bring out the best in other people. It is in these positive relationships that we feel safe and are able to laugh and chuckle freely. For most people, this level of transpersonal (higher) trust is only found with around 5-10 other people. These are your better relationships and they should be nurtured in order to remain vibrant because they help you be your better self. Of course, some people may not have these relationships in their lives and often these are the people who we need to reach out to most.

By what we call 'positive listening', we get to know other people deeply. This is the very essence of good bereavement support, which is all about being kind and encapsulates the concept of 'heads together'. Alongside the individual, community and support groups, public services, such as Social Services, must be effectively delivered with appropriate government investment. What we put into society as individuals, managers and leaders, we do indeed tend to attract back. Positive listening takes a lot of practice. It means actually concentrating, shutting up and really listening. It does not mean listening whilst planning your response. It is not about envy, competition or anger, it is about being really interested in the other person.

Tony Walter, who wrote 'The Revival of Death' (1994 Routledge), my old lecturer at university, in fact (alias Dr Death!), has written extensively and brilliantly on the use of biography when discussing and addressing aspects of death. Of the many books I read whilst studying, this was probably the most useful. It has been interpreted from the sociological, psychological and community perspective. Walter provided somewhat of a paradigm shift, particularly in promoting the usefulness of talking about the lives of the deceased, in order to help with the grieving process. Whilst working as a volunteer or talking with a friend or colleague, I have frequently found it helpful to ask, "So tell me a bit more about..." Individuals have found this emotional pause/extended space helpful, as it can enable them to define the person who they have lost, by the way of biography, as a 'living' person. This is a lovely way to help individuals talk about good experiences they've had, such as holidays and celebrations. It further enables the bereaved to talk about and explore, if they wish, the point of dying, to talk about relationships (with the person and also with their wider circle of family, step-family, friends or colleagues), love, arguments, extended absence, devotion, issues of relief, frustration, hate, loneliness, sadness, joy, ambiguity, finance, unsteadiness and so on. Whether or not someone has experienced a short, absent, secret or long relationship with that person, there is always validation to the story.

At these moments, it is for the bereaved to have the space to fill their stream of consciousness, in any way they define, as long as it is helpful for them. This act of listening is almost transpersonal and is where the grieving individual is listened to, in a way which can be liberating, trusting, safe, open, unburdening and sometimes, very happy. At the end of such conversations, people will often say, "You've really lifted me." At these times, the helper or friend can take comfort in knowing that a conversation may have helped someone. This is perhaps the essence of confluent bereavement care; it is a place where the helper/friend is not absorbed by their own losses, but where they are truly and emotionally 'present' for the other person.

Because I am naturally shy, I am actually more comfortable listening than talking. It is more through nervousness that I might interrupt people! Being more of a listener is a minority trait because it takes a lot of concentration for most people. If, like me, you tend to 'hold things back', concentrate on your trust issues. Not everyone is going to walk away if you decide to reveal something personal about yourself. We all have to take 'risks' and for each one of us, these risks will be different. Sometimes, sharing a bereavement enables a friend to open up too.

On a psycho-dynamic level, it is extremely easy to drift into self-sabotage and into trauma bonds. Trauma bonds are where we regress into behaviours that we feel 'comfortable' with from our childhood. That does not necessarily mean that regression is a good thing. For me, I will regress into 'being the youngest' and act that way, either through charm, frustration, jealousy or resentment. I will also view anger in others as somehow more threatening than it often actually is.

It is also significant where we position ourselves for a photo and how we walk with others. In a classroom, I always sit at the back. This is actually quite common in people who have had to be on 'high alert' during their childhood. By sitting at the back, you can appraise people in front of you and no one can 'strike' you from behind. As suggested before, if you get a chance (and if you haven't got one already), maybe purchase a Fitbit (no promotion intended as there are many other brands available) and observe how much deep sleep you get each night. For young, abused children, sleep is not necessarily a safe place. Some children will have reached adulthood having been on high alert for a high percentage of their lives. These may be individuals who never, without medication or hypnotherapy, achieve a good night's sleep.

———

As Sara Wiseman (in her book 'Heal Your Family Karma') said, "Heal your past, heal your life." Sometimes, the only way that this can be done is through psycho-analytical psychotherapy or through some sort of therapy which is able to 'hold' the difficult feelings within you and guide you through them afresh, in order to come out the other side. It is my view that the 'best' therapy is one that works with your past and brings you along, confluently with your therapist, to the present. Once there (allowing for frequent setbacks and regular analysis), other therapy such as cognitive behavioural therapy, can be sought, in order to get into the knack of 'reframing' sensitive situations.

Cognitive behavioural therapy and counselling is not going to 100% heal your past. However, in moving forwards, Ford (2008) helpfully says, "In taking inventory of some of your life's patterns and lessons, it's not unusual to have feelings that overwhelm anger and even passionate self-determination to arise. Know that you can use these feelings as fuel to get the utmost from the emotion you work on." What she is describing is that your past can make you an even better person, leading you into an insightful and accomplished position. In assessing emotions and stresses, 'shame' is not one of the top emotions that is regularly dissected but, along with pain and loss, in my opinion, shame can be a particularly powerful and destructive emotion.

We also have the issue of gender to consider. Let's be honest here: some women can become 'mean' in their pursuit of power, which is not an attractive trait. Men and women should aspire to work together in a way that breaks down unnecessary power inequalities on both sides. Men have been brought up to 'cope' but they too can be vulnerable. We live in a society where women often want men to be tough and competent one minute, yet tender and sensitive the next. As we map out our lives, these quickly-changing roles are confusing, stressful and bewildering. We are ultimately human beings and there is good and bad in all of us, which is what makes us individuals. Everyone has the capacity to evolve and that should be done in a respectful and understanding way, for both men and women. When it comes to gender and sexual identity, there has been an explosion of labels that some find confusing. Terminology is changing to express a broad spectrum of identities beyond male/female, neutral, man/woman and gay/straight. If we are to become truly 'confluent', we need to let go of some of our traditional labels and become freer, more playful individuals.

One of the most desirable traits is when somebody is and feels they can be their absolute, authentic self. This is usually within 'safe', extremely healthy friendships or relationships. Paradoxically, whilst we are all busy protecting ourselves, we can unconsciously jeopardise our deepest desires and longings. When the 'wounded self' begins to feel secure, we enable ourselves, alongside others, to allow good things into our lives.

Returning to unresolved bereavements, sometimes high achievers, particularly managers and leaders, have experienced what is described as 'strategic survivor personalities'. These are typically the kids sent off to boarding school, or generally brought up by parents who have a high, relentless and academic standard. From the child's feelings of rejection comes a belief that education and success is the resilient starting point. However, in adult life, the ex-boarding school pupil can seem polished and confident, but their ability to connect with or relate to their own emotions and those of other people, is heavily compromised. They may sometimes withdraw from family interactions and try to keep at a safe distance. They may be workaholics who feel they have 'little spare time'.

Typically, but not always, these people have been 'trained' to hold it together and work hard, whilst the rest of us have learnt to just 'collapse' when everything gets too much. With this mindset comes potential vulnerabilities. Connections need to be made in a way that respects each individual's starting point. The advantage of being a 'coper' is that they are trained or wired to hide their vulnerability and be brave. We are all carved out in ways that criss-cross all of these personality trajectories.

On either end of the spectrum, it is important to explore complex emotions, with oneself and others, either at the time or at a later date. It is quite common for children to experience major bereavement traumas without being emotionally 'held' by a parent or carer. The child is too young to have the adult insight into the behaviour around them.

Prince Harry is an example of someone who has undergone self-healing and has publicly demonstrated the positive power of a trained therapist and a supportive partner. Therapists with a knowledge of the military can be particularly useful, as this is a grey area, not easily understood by others. Prince Harry and Meghan are seeking support from each other; the challenge will be whether it is possible to emotionally hold two such difficult public trajectories and channel it into good. Prince Harry indeed publicly stated, "Shutting down all of my emotions for 20 years has had a quite serious effect on my personal and work life… My way of dealing was never to talk about it." Prince Harry perhaps demonstrates that anyone can be susceptible to trauma, loss, anger and resentment. In doing this publicly and supporting the armed forces in such a magnificent way, he has made great strides into making it more acceptable to be male, human and vulnerable.

Additionally, the Duke and Duchess of Cambridge have supported each other publicly, in a mature, insightful, sincere and meaningful way. Their work on mental health, male vulnerability, new mothers and good wellbeing for children, has seen an enormous shift in the paradigm for emotional openness, active listening, nature and fun, around clear support systems.

Boarding schools know that young children can become

extremely upset when their secure attachments (if there were any) to home and loved ones are suddenly ruptured and the staff often work hard to minimise this distress as efficiently as possible. This provides a short-term solution but the emotions often lay buried, ready to emerge at times of huge stress. The way that Prince Harry has channelled his insight and compassion into the success of the Invictus Games is both humbling and impressive. In smaller ways, many individuals who have suffered trauma also choose to help others in need, whether that be by telephone or practical support. The most vulnerable of our society may never be able to get closure with their own family because their trauma is simply too difficult to forgive. Where forgiveness is possible, it does not necessarily mean relationships are improved but it may be a way of freeing oneself from the past. The same can be said for adult relationships and friendships. Forgiveness can be life-changing but needs to be done in a way which does not undermine one's sense of self-worth.

In contrast, the state education sector is performing incredibly well and churning out many well-functioning adults. For some though, the framework of the state system can reinforce 'failure'. Children, from an incredibly young age, are labelled as 'gifted', 'average' or 'weak'. There are also socio-economic, race and health differences to cope with, as well as sibling and peer rivalry. Rivalry, when channelled in a supportive way, can make for small and Olympic achievements. Unfortunately, rivalry can also lead to feelings of inadequacy and self-loathing. I was always fortunate in the secondary state system as I had certain teachers who looked out for me. Teachers are often immensely powerful in installing a sense of resilience. Conversely, teachers who take advantage of young people, even when their emotional or sexual feelings overwhelm them, are unforgivable, for the pain they cause later on. At university level, the dynamic becomes even more complex in this environment, where there are always opportunities for good and also for trauma to be created.

I could not write this book without covering the topic of loss, in the context of social media. Parents may wish to put up 'internet shields' to stop their children going online for too long, in other words, turning the internet off from a certain time. My son still has a little grumble about when I did this for him at 11 years of age. After a few months, I turned it off and he hadn't even realised, as he had automatically accepted the new boundaries! His brain had moulded into the needs of the whole family system. It can also be useful to use apps as a monitoring platform, if it makes you feel more comfortable to see exactly where your child is geographically located. Moreover, passwords need to be shared so that content and material that your children are potentially exposed to can be monitored and feelings can be managed.

The best sex education lessons we can provide to our children is to teach them about morality, humour, respect, boundaries, help sites, appropriate use of smart phones, self-love, the law and other such moral and philosophical discussions. Leave the practical side of things to school but always create an environment where children feel they can talk to you. Bullying is a very real experience for some young people as is poor mental wellbeing, anxiety, depression, competitive pressure, self-harm, economic worth and self-identity. Children do not always 'work it out for themselves' as whatever generation they are from, they remain innocent. They will continue to fumble their way through life where all the tricks need to be practiced and perfected.

For some children, multiple bereavements are a major issue and these inevitably need to be addressed, either at the time or at some point in the future. Loss is not always about a real tangible death. When I worked in the youth justice service, one of my most vulnerable young people was a lad who had an alcoholic mother. Between staying dry and being 'smashed out of her face,' she was always emotionally unavailable. Another lad received an eight-year custodial sentence (at her Majesty's pleasure, thus needing government approval for release), for raping a friend in the woods, a game that had gone horrendously wrong and destroyed a young teenager's life. However, his mother and stepfather visited him, religiously, every week. Despite the seriousness of his crime, they stood by him. Being emotionally available for children is both in the subtle every day and in the more serious of situations. How we talk to and treat our children will have a lasting impact upon them. Even when children are diverted by their peers, in most of these cases, these teenagers will turn out to be well-functioning, working adults. The teen years are one of the most delicate of ages. Do not take your foot off the gas well into independence and if appropriate, always leave your door open for them to return, as young adults.

In 'skipping' (or stumbling, more commonly) along to adulthood, there is always a 'wounded inner child' seeking to get its needs met. This sensitised and emotional radar draws us to certain individuals, groups, jobs and identities. We consciously and unconsciously seek to feed our needs, whether this be through relationships, food or drugs, in fact, everything we do and choose. This can be through financial dependency, ill health or familial pressure. We should take a few minutes each day, whether when watching TV, walking the dog or travelling on public transport, to self-reflect on our choices. With regard to people who have cognitive dependence on us, we should also help them to reflect, if possible and think about how we treat others. When our wounded ego begins to feel safe and secure, we start to allow more good things to happen in our lives.

It is also okay to feel challenging emotions. Nobody is happy all of the time. A happy all of the time place is not an aspirational place to be. Ruby Wax famously said, "It's human to be sad." If something sad has happened, someone has died or we are traumatised, sadness sends a message to our friends to help, allowing us to stop and take stock. Too often we are pressurised to 'feel happy' or to project happy experiences on to social media. *This is not real life.* It is actually quite nice to have a moan sometimes. If you suspect that a child or teenager is being manipulated to feel greater sadness than they actually do, it is important to monitor any potentially harmful sites, such as self-harm and suicide incitement sites. More commonly though, we all have that one group where everything 'is' just SO great. We looked at this earlier and it is about asking yourself, have I got 5-10 friends that I can truly trust and be myself with?

It is important to be straight with yourself and to identify any dysfunctional patterns. We cannot waste our lives blaming others forever, whether that be your manager, sibling, parents, uncle, friend, colleague, therapist or neurologist – the list is endless.

I think here I should mention 'mindfulness'. Mindfulness has its place. At times of great anxiety, it can help us to de-escalate, to visualise and to be thankful. It is particularly good for people who have not had to face too many devastating incidents in their lives. For the most chaotic of people, it can often be helpful. However, it can, if you are talking to someone going through trauma or a recent bereavement, be extremely irritating. 'Being thankful' also has its place, particularly in a spiritual sense, but please note it is sometimes very difficult to be thankful, for even the smallest things, especially if you are homeless, grieving, chronically ill, poor, starving or generally going through great distress.

It is sometimes more useful to explore 'unconcealing'. This is a way of seeing how patterns are replicated (such as view of life, view of race, view of siblings and view of women). With these patterns can come feelings of anger, anxiety and intimidation. Koepke (2019) discusses the issue of strength for both genders: "Being strong means refusing to tolerate people and things that wound your soul. It means practising self-care when you are hurting. It means honouring your feelings by actually allowing yourself to feel and express them. It means treating yourself with compassion and kindness, even when you feel like you do not deserve any. It means doing what makes you happy and being with people who make you feel good. It means asking for help when the weight of the world has become too much." In the context of bereavement, it is important to allow individuals to be vulnerable and ask for help.

It is also about exploring and self-talk. Ore (2019) states, "The real problem isn't that we get rejected (or abandoned, hurt or humiliated) by others. The problem is what we do to ourselves when we get rejected. The problem is what we say to ourselves."

Bowlby (updated 1988) consistently has seen attachment as the secure base from which a child moves out into the world. Over the subsequent years, research has established that having a safe haven promotes self-reliance, confidence, empathy and helpfulness to others in distress. From an incredibly young age, children differentiate themselves from others. Some of the most 'insecure' people we meet in society are completely lacking in these neural, emotional connections or pathways. These are the people that most need our reassurance and time.

The neuroscientist, Joseph LeDoux, and his colleagues have shown that "the only way we can consciously access the emotional brain is through self-awareness, i.e. by activating the medial prefrontal cortex, the part of the brain that notices what is going on inside us and thus allows us to feel what we're feeling. Neuroscience research shows that the only way we can change the way we feel is by becoming aware of our inner experience and learning to 'befriend' what is going on inside ourselves." He advises to work through difficult memories and to breathe deeply so that these memories and feelings can be experienced again in a more manageable way. With practice, this is like completing our own ongoing therapy.

Trauma can emerge in strange ways. Many traumatised

individuals show patterns of hyperactivity the moment they close their eyes: not seeing what is going on around them makes them panic and their brain waves go wild. This is something that I have personally had to manage all of my adult life. Even with relaxation, this is not something that I have been able to manage without medication. It is exceedingly difficult to explain to someone who has not experienced it themselves. It is like a zillion silver flickers on the sky of your eyelids. My brain is alert in sleep, particularly to noise, a sign that the thalamus is having difficulty filtering out irrelevant information.

Ford perfectly articulates the path to healing: "When we come to understand that we are all both good and bad, light and dark, strong and weak, brilliant and oftentimes utterly stupid, we begin the profound process of healing the internal split that invariably takes place for most of us at some time in our lives. This is the only path I've found that actually relieves human suffering. We achieve peace not by learning new tricks or more strategies to hide our imperfections but by embracing more of our insecurities, more of our shame, our fear, and our vulnerabilities." The complexities of the human spirit are what really make people wonderful, complex, quirky, lovable and interesting. She describes each one of us having two inner voices fighting to be heard: the voice of reason, good and conscience and the one of fear, shame and selfishness. She also talks of people aspiring to reach a higher transpersonal level of themselves.

As children, the more trauma that is experienced, through actual traumatic events or constant attack (criticism, put downs or reminders of how rubbish we are), the more that the true 'child spirit' of our personality is lost. This separates us from our true essence. My trauma was that we could not talk in public, even when visiting relatives, without being verbally 'shut down'. It was not until I was 50 years old that I even found out I had a major seizure as a baby. As a result of not even being able to ask the smallest request, I was in effect an elective mute whilst at primary school. As I said before, my friend Kay, who is still a dear friend, spoke for me. Inside I was a bright spark and knew every question being asked by the teachers.

I've also mentioned how when I laugh (and I laugh a lot!), I laugh silently with a sound at the end - my daughter impersonates me perfectly! At 11, humour became my salvation and, of all resilient factors, the ability to laugh should be the most cherished. I find my silent laugh kind of funny and quirky. How sad that the power of laughter can be removed and what greater power is it that it cannot be dampened. We all have a child, a sister or a friend with whom we find ourselves literally rolling around the floor laughing, often to the annoyance of others, or that temptation to make someone laugh at the dinner table. I just cannot resist this one. However hard life gets, embrace your inner child. I have about 10 people in my tribe that make me laugh. I hope they know who they are. A resilience to survive trauma also means that I am able to 'tune in' to other people very well because I had to in order to survive. This has meant that quite a few people think of me as their best friend or certainly that person who would drop everything to drive four hours to them, in their time of need, if that was required. And I would.

During one stressful time, my best friend turned up at my house unannounced. That is quite unusual these days, for non-family members. I still really appreciate that. It is often the little gestures that mean a great deal. Similarly, in other families, children are left too often because their parents are trying to work and do not take the time to get distracted. Living is for today as well as building up for the future. It is a credit to many fathers, not all, but increasingly more than in previous generations, that they often have close relationships with their children. The whole persona of the absent father, the elective non-working father, the unemployed father and the deceased father are all contentious issues around emasculation, power issues and identity issues. It can be a similar case in households where women earn more than their partners do. Life is indeed a combination of the practical and the emotional.

It is often the people who are truly themselves, whatever that may look like, who are the most liked. In order to be our genuine selves, we need to take risks; we need to let our barriers down and if appropriate, we need to let people in, emotionally. People spend years living a false persona and to do this is not to have lived fully. Around this subject is the central ideology of 'denial'. By embracing our flaws and our assets, we set ourselves free to be our true self. By doing so, we may face prejudice and judgement but we should all strive to become our authentic selves.

The healing process for the victim and the victimiser is the same. As children, we are innocent and we become 'moulded' either way. Do not beat yourself up about 'bad' stuff you did. Do not validate it with the insight of adulthood. Vulnerability makes us into more insightful human beings – it is a strength. It is only when we are humanistic that we can truly and genuinely reach out to others.

Forgiveness, if appropriate, is something that we feed ourselves as well as offer to others. It is often surprising the people we hear say they have forgiven, even people who have had a son, daughter, father or friend murdered or some other dreadful deed happen to them. It is not our job to judge these people as everyone should have the freedom to make their own peace. For some, distancing is not enough, they intrinsically need to forgive to set themselves free.

This is also the mindset of peace agreements and historical progress and setbacks. Society emerges and weaves itself in often mysterious and miraculous ways. Sometimes a minority opinion emerges to become a new norm of morality. Consistently, we look to children for opinions as they are often able to reflect without being tarnished by adult economics or practicalities. Forgiveness also plays a part in the every day. It is immensely powerful to apologise to a child, a partner or an employee. It is again about being authentic and mediating to reach a better understanding.

Anger is a powerful emotion, following loss, which sometimes follows us around on our shoulders. When anger has not been resolved, it can unexpectedly undermine us, sometimes constantly, through the day and night. Anger is one of those emotions that, however hard we try, we often can't stop thinking about it. It is the emotion that can consume us, leading to resentment, unresolved issues or offending behaviour, and everyday feelings of irritability, moodiness, gender disharmony, marital issues, lack of self-worth and over-sensitivity. Back in the age of the famous Greek philosophers, Aristotle reflected to his students how important it was "to be angry with the right person, to the right degree, at the right time, for the right purpose, and in the right way." This remains as true today as it was then. Moreover, embracing anger appropriately can enable us to help others. This self-awareness can mobilise us to support others in a meaningful way. This is often the precursor and pre-requisite to assisting, in a voluntary way, in the community or helping a friend or partner.

In his book, 'Emotional Intelligence' (1996), Goleman takes us further back to the evolution of the human being: "From the most primitive root, the brainstem, emerged the emotional centres. Millions of years later in evolution, from these emotional areas evolved the thinking brain or 'neocortex', the great bulb of convoluted tissues that make up the top layers. The fact that the thinking brain grew from the 'emotional' reveals much about the relationship of thought to feeling; there was an emotional brain long before there was a rational one. This gives the emotional centres immense power to influence the functioning of the rest of the brain, including its centre thought. Such emotional explosions are neural hijackings. At those moments, evidence suggests, a centre in the limbic brain proclaims an emergency, recruiting the rest of the brain to its urgent agenda. The hijacking occurs in an instant, triggering this reaction crucial moments before the neocortex, the thinking brain, has had a chance to glimpse fully what is happening, let alone decide if it is a good idea. The hallmark of such a hijack is that once the moment passes, those so possessed have the sense of not knowing what came over them!" During the close connection with emotion and rationality, we have a limited amount of time to take deep breaths and de-escalate. The trick is to work on the interactions of our brains, between thought and feeling if you like, at moments when we are calm and not consumed by basic and sometimes, irrational emotions. This enables us to de-escalate when we feel ourselves getting angry.

We know that the amygdala is busy working archaically and transporting messages to the entire brain. This is necessary in a real human threatening crisis and works simultaneously alongside every nerve and organ of the human body. What is mental is physical and vice versa. In medicine, each part is often assessed separately and the list of tests reinforces this. Many minor physical symptoms could be triaged through to nutritionists, psychotherapists, wellbeing coaches, garden allotment groups, gym supervisors and physiotherapists. Hari states that there is "no evidence that there's a 'chemical imbalance' in the brain of depressed or anxious people." Medication should only be used if it is absolutely essential and the same could be said for vitamin supplements.

Prescribed medication often serves to dull the senses in one way or another. It is perhaps much more useful to explore the life course. Unfortunately, where therapy is proposed, if at all, it is often just a short-term fix. Moreover, it tends to have a cognitive behavioural focus, which only enables the individual to 'reframe' how they are already thinking. This is perhaps useful for smoking cessation or anger strategies but is not usually an appropriate course of action for an individual experiencing multiple traumas. Unfortunately, as Goleman precisely points out, "emotional memories can often be faulty guides to the present." Trauma does not discriminate between rich and poor, man and woman, culture to culture. Trauma is basic to the human experience, only varying in intensity.

Goleman further explores the post-modern idea that people can simply cure themselves and get better. We live in an individualistic society so it is not a surprise that we can be inclined to indirectly blame the individual, as opposed to looking at community or psychoanalytical solutions. When there are good relationships, the experience and recovery from poor health is often evident. Compassion and rapport go a long way. My current GP was able to take away my bereavement anger. This was the most successful, singular achievement of my therapy or 'emotional containment' over the years. Other doctors and nurses, particularly during my miscarriages, were also often extremely compassionate.

There is a saying that anything can be overcome if it is handled in the correct way. This is absolutely true in my view. Emotional experiences follow us through all of our life trajectories. Every interaction with a teacher, child, parent, friend or manager are all significant. Goleman reflects that whilst "some parents are gifted emotional teachers, others are atrocious!" It is never too late to learn strategies. Whilst working in the youth justice system, I witnessed many parents 'improving' their parenting experiences and strategies through effective and well-run parenting programmes. These sorts of programmes are particularly useful for parents not wishing to share knowledge of their children's offending behaviour with their family or friends.

Some discriminated groups such as travellers, offenders, ethnic minorities and the poor are still vilified by society. Change is required to happen at the individual, educational, institutional and political levels to properly take full effect. Expressing an opinion, directly or on social media, is never enough.

Within society, there can sometimes be a subconscious imbalance of power. Hugman (1991) focuses on the relationships between caring professionals and service users or patients. In this context, patients are frequently at the mercy of what doctors assess as the best 'medicine' or plan of action. This may not be in quite the order that the patient wishes but ultimately, the doctor will have the decision-making power. When you take risks and step outside your traditional patterns of behaviour, new opportunities can arise. Mutual trust can result in a more equal and genuine working relationship between the professional and the patient.

Sigmund Freud famously said, "I think this man or woman *[sic]* is suffering from memories. When exploring the past, many traumatised individuals are haunted by the shame they feel about what they themselves did or did not do under (certain) circumstances." Van Der Kolk (2014) describes how individuals sometimes despise themselves and can have "feelings of terror, dependency, excitement and anger…whether that be at home or in an institution." She says how "numbing and trauma changes people's perception and imagination." It is no wonder that individuals become ill because of 'burying' these sensations and feelings into adulthood. She was often surprised, in the course of her work, "by the way patients' symptoms were discussed and by how much time was spent on trying to manage their symptoms, rather than understanding the possible causes of their despair and helplessness." She was struck by how little time was paid to their accomplishments and aspirations, whom they cared for, loved or hated, what motivated them and engaged them, what kept them stuck, and what made them feel at peace, the ecology of their lives. Several writers have described how the 'best' stories are told by patients during the night at mental health establishments or in the cars of social workers. It seems obvious that we should focus on what makes people tick and work from there. As a practitioner, it is useful to ask, "What happened to you?"

For better or worse, many people have been trained to believe that openly communicating, in a clear and honest way, won't get them what they want. This is generally a mistake. They have learnt to play games or go on power trips. Moreover, entire families play out scripts, often falling into roles which everyone knows about, but no one mentions. Families are also well known to fill spaces or vacancies. It is unusual to have two leaders in a family or two extroverts/introverts. People frequently slip into a role that is going to fit. Families that have all leaders often come unstuck and are unwilling to step down or compromise. Where conversations are just around who can win petty arguments, it is often irrelevant 'buzz'. Where there are numerous children, parents/carers can split children into the 'good' child and the 'bad' child. This can be very damaging for children. Similarly, children can attempt to split parents to meet their own needs. At no greater time is it essential as parents to be a united team. In stepfamilies, children sometimes do this very successfully and will mark 'success' not just on their emotional needs being met but their commercial (electronic) means being met too.

Elrod (2016) in 'The Miracle Morning' looks at some useful self-help strategies which I have listed and adapted here:

Silence
Sit in silence, praying, meditating and focusing on breath, for ten minutes. Debbie describes her stress melting away and a sense of calm coming over her body and an easing of her mind. She describes moving from chaos to peacefulness.

Reading
Debbie spends 10 minutes reading motivational literature. Many therapists will tell you that if you start your day well, it will often continue that way. Negativity on the other hand projects

throughout the day, from being late, to being moody, to arguing with a colleague, to shouting, being tired or late for dinner. Start the day well!

Affirmations

Debbie jotted down what she wanted, who she was committed to being and what she was committed to doing to change her life. This can be something small or something major. It may mean you intend to talk to someone in a different way, use positive praise to get the best out of your child or it may be something bigger. Everybody's story and path is different. To aspire to 'be true to yourself' in your decision-making is a good start!

Visualisation

This is the idea to close your eyes and picture something that calms you down. I always use the face of my dogs as they give me unconditional love and always make me smile. The power of animals or nature is positive and therapeutic.

Journaling

Debbie described how the simple act of writing things down 'lifted' her.

Exercise

Walking 10,000 steps a day will have a positive impact on your life. If doing this 'stuff' means getting up at 5am, do it. The middle of the night or the early hours are some of the most amazing times of the day. I remember feeding my first born at 3am and loving the special time of just me and Max. My baby group friends found this impossible to understand!

Elrod states, "If 95% of our society is not living the life that they want, we must figure out what they did wrong or what they didn't do right, so that we don't end up living a life of mediocrity." She continues, "We don't want our lives to be a struggle. We want a life of freedom, where we get to wake up and do what we want, when we want, with whomever we want. We want to get out of bed every day and truly love life. We want to love work and love the people we get to share our life and work with. That is my definition of success. That kind of life does not just happen. It must be designed. If you want to live an extraordinary life as defined and designed by you, then you must identify the fundamental causes of mediocrity so you can prevent them from robbing you of the life you want." We need to explore what this means for ourselves.

So how did some of these insights further help me on my journey?

Let us re-examine trauma. Paradoxically, I really loved and trusted my father. I was his 'youngest and least threatening' (clearly my brother was the 'bad' child, which was a terrible abuse of my father's power). For my father, my brother was a huge disappointment. I adore the purity of my brother with his learning disability but sadly, it was a different era. I accepted the label of youngest, favourite, 'the pretty one,' as it served to protect me and enabled me to have some sense of worth. I always knew my father would have my back. I also figured out from an incredibly early age that he was stressed due to his bereavement trauma. This was not something that was hidden from me and in some, partly damaged way, this has enabled me to be insightful and self-aware. In theoretical texts, this relationship would be known as a 'trauma bond': a bond or relationship that someone is 'attracted' to but where it is not in any shape or form a healthy attachment. Attachment is therefore neither secure nor insecure but a kind of manipulated magnet. My childhood (feminists, do not scream!) taught me to be absolutely charming, to everyone. In some ways, this sounds manipulative but I like to see it as a nice characteristic. I know exactly how to make friends, keep people on board and show loyalty.

My father was an academic man and highly intelligent. He passed on to me his intellectual and trauma genes and sometimes, his anger. What I loved most about him though was his love of gardening and nature. As Alice Walker affirms, "Never go past the colour purple in the field without noticing it." The beauty around us is nourishing and feeds our soul. Some people, at the end of a busy day, enjoy some quiet and meditative time, in their gardens. This is a way to unwind, de-escalate, think and reflect. Small research projects have also demonstrated the benefit of garden allotment and outdoor projects.

The power of nature allows our blood pressure to lower and to appreciate our own happy place. If we look into nature, in deep thought, we often 'find' what we are looking for. My father, like me, was able to write about and enjoy gardening and nature more articulately than he could speak. For someone so damaged, he was able to write beautiful poetry and communicate loving words through writing and growing flowers and vegetables. Human beings are complex creatures: love and hate can sometimes be intricately linked. Writing thoughts and feelings down can be extremely helpful if you have suffered bereavement. I personally have a bereavement list and messages, in the notes pages of my iPhone, to keep all my losses in one place. This enables me to think about them, occasionally, in a more manageable way. Without it, there are just too many losses to conjure up in one thought process.

There is sometimes a link between childhood trauma and neurological symptoms, especially if a child's needs have not been met or they have been emotionally abandoned; the body can go into panic/escape mode. Do not expect a neurology patient to act 'normally'. They may be experiencing tingling, dizziness, faintness, numbness, pain, anxiety, shivers, high blood pressure, palpitations, and more. They may not smile at you. It does not mean they are not happy. They need timely and appropriate investigations. They sometimes need to be asked, "How have things been?" Or "What happened to you?" Rather than, "What are your symptoms?"

One of the most helpful things I recently achieved was to mostly give up alcohol. It never agreed with me anyway! Once my acupuncturist asked me, "Why do you drink if it makes you feel faint?" I explained that I was attempting to 'get my body used to it'. Even I wasn't convinced!

As of today, I still do not have a satisfactory diagnosis within my body, apart the presence of a cavernoma. Functional neurological disorders (FND) are often deemed to be based on psychological reactions to past social experiences, and biological and genetic predisposition. These stereotypical and ambiguous explanations usually result in patients feeling alienated, stigmatised and even not believed. I sincerely hope that people are believed, with every word they say, and that *all* areas of healthcare are one day treated equally. People with neurological disorders, or symptoms, often feel that they don't have a voice. Listen to them carefully, believe them, 'feel them', understand their pathways, do not judge, do not question, for it is not 'all in their heads'. Even though my symptoms have been labelled as FND by the medical professionals, I find that people can identify more easily with the concept of a cavernoma because it is a tangible diagnosis. This is somewhat ironic because I truly believe that my cavernoma does contribute to my neurological symptoms.

If something does not look right to you, do not post it on social media. Instead, be kind, talk, reach out and feel the inner pain. Whatever your journey, view others with compassion and without question. Overcoming our own backgrounds and emotional battles perhaps puts us all in a good position to trust and genuinely reach out to others.

Functional neurological disorder just means that you have various symptoms but the cause, following tests, has not been found yet. Keep questioning. Do not be put off by being viewed as 'a nuisance'. It is *your* health, *your* body and *your* mind – you own it. Reach out and give love despite the fight. Do not give up because it is not all in your head. Believe in yourself: you, as the patient, know your mind pretty well.

_____

"Those who are grieving need us. They need you."

Cruse Bereavement Care

_____

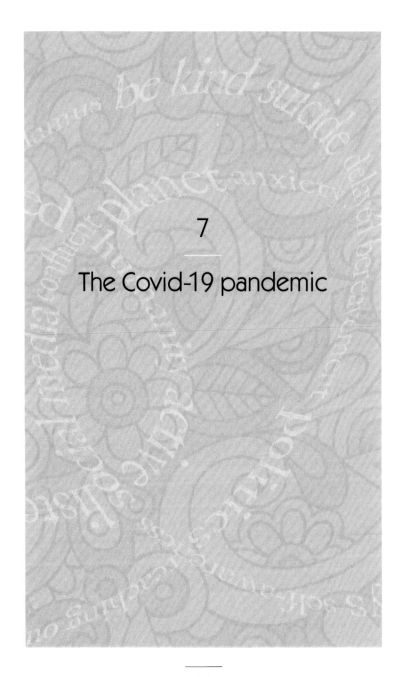

7

The Covid-19 pandemic

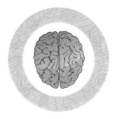

Covid-19 has had an enormous impact in shifting the 'heads together' and 'being kind' messages. Communities have united and communities have split. The political became the personal. It was a time that brought out the best and worst in people.

It is 2020. The year when, having a few months off school, helped many children to rest and heal emotionally and we realised perhaps that good mental health was even more important than academic achievement – or at least, just as important. Yet we must also acknowledge that for traumatised children, it could have been a very frightening and overwhelming time. In one way or another, the entire world has been traumatised, to a lesser or greater degree, by the pandemic. Keyworkers went from being admired in some areas of work and vilified in others. The world was coming apart at the seams.

My husband had been put on the 12-week lockdown to protect his own health needs (he has weak lungs and previous cancer of the throat) and we were all initially on full lockdown in the UK, apart from being able to take two hours of socially-distanced exercise outside each day. Coming out of lockdown, the country was splintered and suffering. Emotions were raw and the media sometimes manipulated the news, creating greater divisions.

During this time, I became acutely aware of the impact of health and trauma on a national level. Hats off to Chris Whitty, Chief Medical Officer and health advisor to No. 10, who also recognised that there were many people whose 'normal' healthcare needs had been deferred. This was partly because the healthcare requirements of the country were assessed in a reactive way, in difficult times, based on their physical rather than mental health and wellbeing. The entire world was going through trauma. This very trauma, fear and anxiety that normally occurs on a micro level, was now expanding on a macro level.

Trust is about trusting our leaders, which at times was challenging and at other times, admirable. The world was opening its eyes to vulnerability in terms of health, death and trauma. New conversations took place and strangers were helping each other. Doctors and nurses were placed under tremendous pressure. Teachers were initially unnecessarily vilified for not being seen to 'step up,' when they were working extremely hard, doing everything they could. Shop workers and refuse collectors were thanked. Social workers were hardly acknowledged, despite many losing their lives to Covid-19. Keyworkers were ultimately given celebrity status as society's moral compass changed. The traditional celebrities were either strangely quiet or openly politicising.

Covid-19 has precipitated, for the first time in the postmodern era, the exploration of joint trauma, joint connections and joint restorative solutions. Vaccines, treatments and vulnerabilities have been investigated. Most importantly, 55,000 people had tragically died of Covid-19 at the time of writing this book, mainly during the first wave of the virus.

We then were able to tentatively rediscover our lost freedoms in the autumn of 2020 but it came at the cost of a second wave. Will there be a greater mutation return next year? We are unable to go within two metres of people beyond our immediate family. Would winter bring good or bad news? Furthermore, how do we 'connect' without touch? The use of social media was mastered by many!

At no other time has there been a greater need for the joint endeavour of community; people supporting each other; being kind; heads together; and for the active promotion of bereavement and loss support services.

You will be understanding the underlying theme of 'be kind' and 'heads together' by now. By being honest, undertaking active listening skills, keeping to timeframes, hearing the story from the patient's perspective, being genuine, writing clear letters, reviewing promises, understanding trauma and so forth, is what is at the heart of being more humanistic. Giddens (1992) describes the 'confluent relationship'. He talks about romantic relationships but similarly all relationships should be based upon mutual respect and understanding rather than be fixed by outdated norms of power and gender differentiation.

Confluence is perhaps one person benefitting from another in a pure way where neither feels exploited and both feel their needs and views have been met. Based upon this premise is the desired investment in healthcare so that all can benefit, at a micro and macro level. The NHS, voluntary groups, individuals and local groups potentially epitomise the foundations for which this can be organised and achieved.

———————

"If you can't be kind, be quiet."

Author unknown

———————

8

Reaching out to
the bereaved

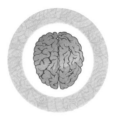

The Duke and Duchess of Cambridge have been inspiring in sending out the immensely powerful message that it is important to talk. Moving beyond this, to an almost transpersonal level, is the importance to listen. For every case of 'it's all in your head', there will be some element of trauma.

I hope that there will be a recognition, at government level, that mental health services are going to need a huge future investment to support those with bereavement and pandemic trauma. Individuals with these issues are perhaps the most vulnerable in our society, so telling them that it's all in their head is unhelpful.

Our world is grieving. We do need to be strong and positive but we also urgently need wider psychodynamic services and training so that we are truly able to listen to people. It's about the collective, the connection of people around the world. It is the coming together of being human, first and foremost. It transcends worth, occupation, social standing, poverty and inequality: the human experience is about showing human vulnerability, joint support and potential for positive community action. That strength cannot be found in individuals alone, it is about reconnecting as a community. How we connect and develop relationships is intrinsically linked to our upbringing: some of those relationships will be harmful but some will be incredibly powerful.

Trust needs to be earned and human beings need to be understood with compassion. Take the time to understand why someone is kicking off, listen to the patient's perspective, listen to your friend, your partner, reach out to your communities, volunteer, care and be kind. It is not material possessions that ultimately make us happy, it is the pleasure in helping others so that they can find their individual way forward. Always see humour in whatever place you find yourself because humour, if appropriate, is the best medicine. Acknowledge, reach out, laugh, get help and keep well.

We can also learn from other cultures. It will probably be some considerable time before we are able to travel again. The 'gap year' may temporarily become a non-entity. But looking at other cultures I've experienced such as Morocco, Thailand and Iceland, we can see how people comfortably communicate and help each other. This was never truer than in Iceland when the cheap and unsuitable tent that my sister and I were staying in blew away. The locals came to our aid, without us asking, and put us into a local community centre building for a few days. The men regularly came and visited us to check we were alright but we were extremely nervous, fearing that we would be mugged or raped! It was in fact a selfless act of genuine, community support. When I travelled again with the same sister across Morocco, during Ramadan, people were quick to share their late evening food with us, even when they had little themselves. Giving to others invariably gives us more pleasure than to receive. Religions such as Islam, Hinduism and Buddhism have some valuable lessons to teach us about love and sharing.

The modern world needs us to peel away the fake programmes, fake eyebrows, fake bodies, fake nails and masks, to explore what is fundamentally at the inner core of the human endeavour. Men and women are inherently different but, in some ways, the same. Moving forwards, we should always look towards bringing the issue of gender together, as at times, there appears to be some conflict. We need to understand the term 'confluent living' , where people live side by side, in a respectful and aligned fashion.

It is not steeped in old gender stereotypes and there is a regard to what the 'other' brings to the relationship. It is pure and loving on a humanistic level, recognising the general differences between men, women and all human beings. We are all indeed citizens of the world.

Every relationship has its own timeline, its own purpose and its own lessons to teach. Even the most difficult relationships exist to help us learn and grow. Relationships sometimes change and at a certain point, we realise we have to come to terms with what has occurred, good or bad.

Open spaces and gardens can be very restorative. During Covid-19, many people reconnected with nature, some perhaps just wishing to escape the lockdown! Now is a time to 'connect,' not just with people but with the world and nature around us. Nature has spoken.

I found a Facebook quote (author unknown), which resonated with me and I think it really sums up the whole concept of bereavement support, being kind and 'heads together':

"If you're thankful, show it. If you love someone, tell them. If you're wrong, fess up. If you're confused, ask questions. If you learn something, teach others. If you're stuck, ask for help. If you made a mistake, apologise. If you trip, get back up. If someone needs help, help them. If you see wrong, take a stance."

This seems to me a good starting point to live by.

—————

"Know that deep inside, you are resilient, brave and so much stronger and more powerful than your fears."

Gail Lynne Goodwin

—————

9

Practical approaches

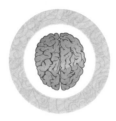

So far, we have learnt that by understanding somebody's life story, we are more likely to be emotionally available for them. This is the essence of the charities 'Cruse Bereavement Care' and 'Heads Together'. To then actively listen is to take support to the next level. Being kind is showing humanity to those close to us and to strangers too. It is working towards the common good, maintaining fair policies and treating people, whether they are seen as 'good' or 'bad,' with the same unconditional regard.

We need to approach trauma in a sensitive way. For example, if someone has a miscarriage, we say, "I'm so sorry" and acknowledge the loss to both parents. Bueno said, "Choosing to remember is not a neutral choice. The commitment to remember, especially in the face of subtle and not so subtle pressures to forget, is clearly understood by bereaved parents to be an honourable, moral choice." Whatever trauma someone is relaying, listen and believe them. Active listening skills are perhaps the most useful therapeutic tool we all hold. Do not plan the next sentence in your head but truly be there, in the moment, and let the person take as much time as is needed.

Loss is a common trauma and can happen on many different levels: loss of parenthood, loss through illness, loss of a job, loss of a marriage, a relationship, a pet, anything in which someone is left empty and hurting. 'Cruse Bereavement Care' notes that "people react to loss in different ways. Talk to people, don't let your hurt grow until you break down." Similarly, if you think someone is hurting or you can see it coming, be there! If someone is suffering mentally, do not shy away from bringing up the subject. You will soon get the message if someone doesn't wish to talk about it. Initiate conversations to try and make someone's day special.

'Mental Health England' outlines how mental wellbeing affects us all, on a swinging point. We all have protective factors, such as family, professionals, access to services, pets, supportive employees and we all have negatives: stress, grief, reduced social interaction, physical illness, low self-esteem, housing access, to name a few. We all have 'emotional containers', some smaller or bigger than others, which sometimes overflow. Specific signs to look out for include withdrawal, distress, drinking more, tearfulness, panic attacks or distorted thinking. Look out for signs of post-traumatic stress and self-harm. Statistically, there are on average 16 suicides per day in the UK, 75% male and 25% female. The 50-60 age group is actually the biggest but it is also depressingly high for those in their twenties, with suicide accounting for a significant proportion of those deaths. Do not be afraid to ask someone straight how they are feeling.

So, how else do you approach someone who is suffering? Keep positive, be yourself, keep body language open, be empathetic. Do not advise or diagnose! Ask how they are feeling at that moment, and how long they have felt like that. Ask if there is anything you can do to help. Accept that it is real for them. Try and get on their wavelength and see things from their perspective. Look at their body language. Assess whether they need to talk to someone professionally or if they are at immediate risk. Do you think you need to call 999 or are you comfortable that you have it under control? Are they acting out of the ordinary? Have work or personal relationships changed? Try and feel comfortable with difficult discussions. At the same time, remain self-aware and look after yourself too; listening to people can sometimes be shocking and stressful. Do not underestimate the effect this may have on you. What can you do to maintain your emotional resilience? Maybe things like talking, texting, exercising, working, or journaling. Being able to listen to somebody else's distress and remain resilient and non-judgemental is an art that needs much work.

As well as looking after yourself and those in obvious need, also try and look after the people who seem okay. It is sometimes difficult to know who may need help or support, but we all do really, whether or not we show it. We sometimes do not even realise it ourselves, such is the level of subconscious denial or the desperate need to appear to be coping and managing. Some people will go through an entire day without someone genuinely asking if they are okay.

Self-esteem is powerful to the human psyche, essential to our life purpose; healthy self-esteem enables us to function properly as adults. What can we do as parents, carers or step-parents, in order to build up self-esteem in children, in a practical way? This is useful advice for all parents but particularly so for children who witness marital breakdown, violence, emotional abuse, alcohol and drug problems, or who experience bullying, housing and/or educational moves.

Here are some positive phrases and affirmations that may help:

- I love you.
- I enjoy spending time with you.
- I like the way…
- I like you because…
- You made a great effort.
- You did well on…
- I hear your anger.
- Would you like to tell me more?

- I believe you.
- I am interested in what you think.
- You are enough as you are.
- I am able to listen to sensitive, difficult, angry or embarrassing subjects and feelings.

Regarding healing, we must remember that avoiding people who cause you to trigger is not always the answer. Transformation happens when you are triggered but you are still able to self-manage the pain, deconstruct the triggers and move forward in an insightful and more self-aware way.

Lidenfield (2000) has identified these helpful tips and strategies to deal with emotion.

What do we mean by self-awareness?

- Recognise and name your own emotions.
- Understand the causes of feelings.
- If appropriate, move feelings into actions.

Managing emotions

- Become more tolerant and de-escalate your anger.
- Do not overstep boundaries.
- Avoid verbal put-downs, fights and unnecessary 'buzz'.
- Express anger calmly and don't get personal.
- Respect other people's viewpoint.
- Avoid pushing people away.
- Embrace positive feelings about self, partners (if appropriate) and colleagues.
- Be better at handling stress. Ask questions.
- Do not assume the worst.
- Work on loneliness and take action for help with social anxiety.

What are the typical feelings that sit alongside emotions?

Anger: fury, outrage, resentment, wrath, exasperation, indignation, animosity, annoyance, irritability, hostility and perhaps at the extreme, pathological hatred and violence.

Sadness: moodiness, grief, sorrow, negativity about others, gloom, melancholy, self-pity, loneliness, dejection, despair and when pathological, severe depression.

Fear: anxiety, apprehension, nervousness, concern, consternation, misgiving, wariness, edginess, dread, fright, terror; as a psychopathology, phobia and panic.

Enjoyment: happiness, joy, relief, contentment, bliss, delight, amusement, pride, sensual pleasure, thrill, rapture, gratification, satisfaction, euphoria, laughter, ecstasy and at the far edge, mania.

Love: acceptance, confluence with others, friendliness, freedom within, trust, kindness, affinity, devotion, adoration, infatuation, enjoyment, joy and pleasure.

Surprise: shock, astonishment, amazement and wonder.

Disgust: contempt, disdain, scorn, abhorrence, aversion, distaste, revulsion or hate.

Shame: guilt, embarrassment, remorse, humiliation, regret, mortification and self-loathing.

What are our cognitive skills?

- Self-talk: effective and insightful self-dialogue.
- Reading and interpreting social cues: looking at body language, accepting rejection.
- Using steps for problem-solving and decision-making: behaving appropriately, sensitively and morally, controlling impulses, setting goals, identifying alternative actions, anticipating consequences. Being honest with people and avoiding unnecessary hurt or surprise.

- Understanding the perspective of others, even if it is different to your own. Agreeing and validating others, if appropriate.
- Understanding how to be a reliable and loving friend.
- Having a positive attitude towards life.
- Self-awareness: understanding yourself and the impact you have on others.

Behavioural skills

- Nonverbal: communicating through eye contact, facial expressiveness, tone of voice, gestures, smiling, leaning inwards, mirroring others.
- Verbal: making clear requests (without being bossy), responding effectively to criticism, resisting negative influences, listening to others, helping others, participating in positive peer groups, telling people that they have hurt or confused you.
- Handling stress: learning the value of exercise, guided imagery and relaxation methods.
- Personal responsibility: taking responsibility, recognising the consequences of your decisions and actions on yourself and others, accepting your feelings and moods, and following through on commitments. Having the ability to apologise sincerely when you have done something wrong.

How can we bring children up in a resilient way?

This section is slightly subjective as everyone has their own ideas about effective parenting. I therefore own it as my personal view on effective parenting. By a 'parent,' this can be any primary individual(s) who are socialising children in their care.

How do we deliver on the development of self-love, self-awareness, goal setting and positivity? How do we allow children the freedom to express themselves in all areas of the emotional spectrum?

Lindenfield (2000) suggests the following ways to communicate effectively with children.
Don't be afraid to continue with these strategies into the teenage years and adulthood, if appropriate. Positive praise, for example, "I like it when you…" works very well with teens.

Share positive feelings

I love you.
I love being with you.
I am enjoying playing this game with you.
I love reading to/with you.
I care so much about you.
You have given me so much joy.
I get such a kick out of spending time with you.
I felt proud when I saw you doing…
I was so moved when…
I felt so appreciated by you when you…
I felt so proud of you when I read…
I felt so excited to be seeing you again…

Specify appreciation

I like the way you…
I like you because…
You are very important to me because…
You have a special talent for…
You are individual.
I like your smile.
You sing with feeling.

You're fun because…
You're so creative! Just look at the way…
You were witty without being hurtful.
Congratulations on the way…
You're a really good friend – look at the way you…
I would love to have you over because…
You look great. You have a good sense of colour.
Thank you for…
You deserve it because…
I admired the way…

Recognise effort and achievement

You worked really hard on that.
I know you were doing your best.
That's an amazing achievement - well done! You have…
Since last week, I have noticed a vast improvement…
Look at the progress you have made…
Your talent really showed when you…
You should feel proud…

Convey unconditional acceptance

I accept that you are cross with me for…
I know you get in bad moods sometimes but…
I can understand you may feel jealous.
It's okay for you to make mistakes.
You don't have to be perfect all the time.
I know you can be aggressive, but you can also be…
There are times when I get mad but I still love you.

Confirm trust

I trust you to…
I have every faith in you.
I know you can do it.
You're a winner.
You'll work it out, if anyone can.
I can always count on you.
I know you'll cope but if it's tricky, that's okay.
I am relying on you.
I'd like to ask your opinion.
I really value your judgement.
I'd like you to help me with…
What do you think?

Here, are some of my further suggestions.

Acknowledge trauma

Would you like to talk about…
You look thoughtful?!
I enjoyed it when we used to spend time with…
How are you feeling on a scale of 0-10?
What would need to change to make things feel different?
Is there anything I can do to help?
Shall we purchase a pet for you to look after?
I miss… do you?
Have you anything you wish to put on the worry bus?
Shall we rub your feet and have a chat?
Let's paint your nails (and talk).
Has anyone ever told you to keep a secret?

Communicating with adults

Would you like me to come to the appointment with you?
I love you as a friend because…
I miss you.
I appreciate you because…
You're a great friend because…
Shall we go out to play (enter activity) ?
Shall we plan this together…
Can I help in any way?
Let's chat!
Do you miss…
How are you feeling about…
Every step is an achievement.
I'm proud of you.
I accept you as you are.

Dunn Buron (2007) explores the escalation of boundaries, as listed below:

1. Very informal social behaviour
2. Reasonable behaviour
3. Odd behaviour
4. Scary behaviour
5. Physically hurtful or threatening behaviour

The book is very good and contains some useful work sheets on emotion. It can sometimes be confusing for young adults to know what is okay and what is not okay. This is written in an accessible way that both a teenager or parent would easily understand. It sets out clearly how young people should behave, if they wish to be perceived positively and appropriately.

"The final stage of healing is using what happens to you to help other people."

Gloria Steinem

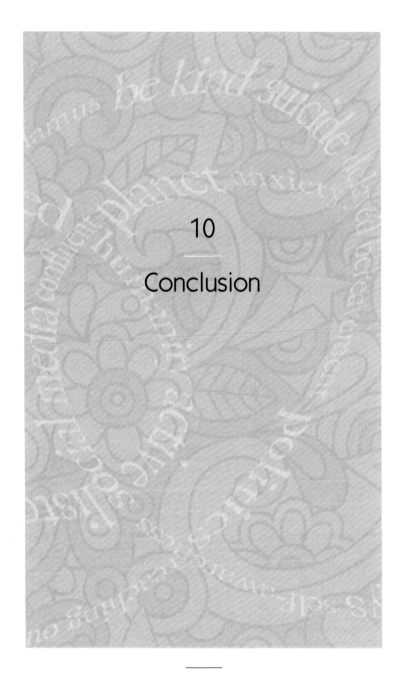

10

Conclusion

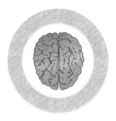

The conclusion to this book is about new beginnings. We have explored in great detail what bereavement and trauma can do to the human mind and body. From the meeting of minds through to the understanding of trauma, to practical strategies for being kind, this book will hopefully sit alongside and complement many other good books, established by formal companies, voluntary organisations and good human beings. We really are all in this together. These values plant the seeds to reconnect with people, nature and our planet Earth. The conversations have started and immobilisation, on the micro and macro level, is starting to take shape.

The most important thing is to start a conversation. From here, wonderful things can take place. This results in people potentially being able to help you and similarly, you being able to help others. This sense of interconnection is what makes for a healthy, mentally aware and highly functioning, emotional society. I particularly respect how Prince William spends time focusing on men's mental health. Together, men and women can become 'confluent' and complement each other's similarities and differences. The Duke and Duchess of Cambridge epitomise a progressive way forward, for us and our children. We are potentially at the beginning of a more positive, humanistic and better world.

We have learnt that good mental wellbeing is important, and I have demonstrated ways to re-connect, through specific strategies. By reaching out to others, we do truly get to live our lives in fuller, more vibrant ways. When we feel more connected with one another and nature, we start to repair ourselves and are more in harmony with the universe around us.

Firstly, we explored various examples of childhood bereavement trauma, where poor mental health can emerge. It is only when we hear the unique stories of ourselves and others that we can 'reach in' to help ourselves and in turn, 'reach out' to help others.

During my childhood, like many, there were layers and layers of daily trauma. This has a cumulative effect and you have no time to process it and heal before the next trauma occurs. We explored the very heart of trauma and the origins of bereavement on the neural pathways, discussing how we can truly connect and 'see' the path that we, and others, have travelled. We then explored the teenage years, the era of social media and the need to protect our children.

We extrapolated the powerful impact of loss and how each bereavement can make the next bereavement even harder. This took our insight into connectivity even further. We looked at being kind in the context of suggesting practical questions to ask individuals, including children, teenagers and adults.

We explored the importance of respecting the unique nature of bereavement, as everyone comes with a new trajectory, all slightly different. Using trauma as a basis to understand pain, we can become better equipped to repair ourselves and the relationships around us. We explored issues of expectation and guilt, damaged relationships and recovery. We examined the way the brain works and how it affects the body and our behaviour. We learnt to be kind to ourselves and others and not to have too high expectations, other than to survive, function, adjust to a new norm and then to potentially heal and flourish. We acknowledged that we are both individual but also connected to others in our grief. We considered the confluent relationship whereby we sit, supportively, alongside one another.

We looked at sociological factors such as living in a household with a sibling with disabilities, homelessness, gender, ethnicity and identity and how these factors can impact our self-worth. We proposed how to instil resilience and maintain good mental wellbeing even when faced with bad experiences. We explored the rapidly changing expectations of gender identity and how a 'shift' was needed away from old stereotypes.

We also went on a health journey and looked at the links between 'good' and 'bad' health and wellbeing. This led to an exploration of 'good' and 'bad' relationships, in different parts of the book, with regard to parents, health staff, siblings, friends and partners. We looked at how these relationships can affect self-worth, identity and self-esteem. We explored how 'good' relationships can be confluent, mutually beneficial and joyful. We learnt how to stick with difficult feelings or people and how to become more self-aware.

We explored health structures, organisations and power and looked at which relationships assist patients to emotionally 'heal'. We looked at the impact of missed diagnosis, delays and also the importance of validating symptoms and receiving a diagnosis, if appropriate. This section is to provide insight rather than criticism. We can all make mistakes and the importance is to learn from them.

We looked at how our own parenting approaches are influenced by our own trauma and loss journeys. Personality types were examined in detail, in order to further assist self-awareness. We explored the typical traits of traumatised adults, so that we can be more in touch with others. We looked at the many ways and techniques to help one another. We also covered the importance for acknowledging the impact of trauma and bereavements, self-love, self-development, relaxation techniques and self-help.

Our individual lives and how we can realistically lead them, are interwoven with how we treat the planet Earth. This can be an immensely powerful tool, when thinking about the connection between personal loss, human degeneration and world loss and extinction. Making these connections and acting upon them can be very powerful. For example, converting our homes to environmentally friendly components, using an e-bike or walking more and using a car less, giving up or reducing air flight, buying sustainable clothes, turning off lights, eating in a responsible way, gardening, recycling, picking up rubbish, and so forth. It creates a healthy state of living and a holistic healing process. Saving both ourselves and our planet are closely intertwined. Developing beyond the confluent and saving ourselves, jointly, takes us to the next level, our endeavour to stop our planet dying.

Covid-19 perhaps woke the world up to a new beginning. It has been a reflective time for us all and we had to find inner strength, as we were either pushed into lockdown or pushed to the front line. Death stared us starkly in the face, for some, literally, and for many, through the media. There was never a more important time to reach out. We were forced to consider the challenges that were being faced on an individual, community and political level. At no other time, since World War II, had there been such a feeling of solidarity. A minority struggled to comply, and we analysed why, but what was evident was an outpouring of 'community love'. Trauma and inequality were palpable and it was no longer possible to ignore the stark realities of the inequality of this virus, through homelessness, economic ruin, national bankruptcy and a propensity to Covid-19 itself.

A new dawn had awakened. The planet itself needed protection and better management. The environment has had the opportunity to have some rest and recuperation, reflected by smog dramatically reducing on our planet, but much more healing is needed. Individuals also needed to take responsibility. Humans were no longer the leaders in the world playground. New ideologies emerged to replenish the environment. We are indeed aspiring to and reaching out for a better, more connected, higher transpersonal place of being.

There are encouraging murmurings about a Covid-19 vaccine that justify cautious optimism. Researchers should know whether the experimental vaccine has worked by the end of the year. Even if a vaccine is found and we manage to eradicate the virus, the world and our reality as we know it has fundamentally altered.

Covid-19 has had a crippling effect on the world economy and unemployment rates are increasing daily. The efforts of the medical profession turned towards prioritising the pandemic and the consequences of this are still being felt in other areas of healthcare, with the postponement of screening, diagnoses, treatment programmes and operations. On a personal level, I was seen by my GP for my mental wellbeing and screened for gynaecological issues during Covid-19 within the two-week urgent referral window. My husband also required some tests and has been referred within the target timelines. I know others who have also been seen in Hampshire but not everyone in the country has been so fortunate. These wider concerns have largely been down to Covid fear (from the patient) and prioritisation, in good faith (from the government and the varying professionals).

On a sociological and emotional level, loneliness and general reduced social contact has added to the pressure on mental wellbeing, depression and anxiety. The individuals who have been particularly valued during these challenging times are health and care workers, regular delivery drivers, shop workers and volunteers. This is partly due to the intrinsic human and animal need for social contact. Loneliness in the UK has soared as the number of people feeling isolated and alone rose from 2.6 million before the Covid crisis to a peak of 4.2 million within six months. However, Zoom and similar apps have been useful for many.

On a personal, community and political level, what values,

insights and changes will you take with you, in the post-Covid era?

Life's challenges will never go away and the after effects of Covid-19 could be with us for many years to come. Yet hopefully, what the pandemic has taught us is to practice kindness and compassion. We can take comfort in human beings merging together and finding a way to exist in times of need. We are indeed aspiring and reaching out for a more connected and liberated place of being. We are already working towards or living at the transpersonal and 'confluent' level.

_____

"Love and compassion are necessities, not luxuries. Without them, humanity cannot survive."

Dalai Lama

_____

References and further reading

Attenborough, David (2020) *"A Life on Our Planet: Witness Statement and a Vision for the Future"*, Ebury Digital.

Bowlby, John (1988) *"A Secure Base: Clinical applications of Attachment Theory (revisited)"*, Psychology Press.

Bueno, Julia (2019) *"The Brink of Being: Talking About Miscarriage"*, Virago.

Byrne, Rhonda (2006) *"The Secret"*, Simon & Schuster UK.

DailyOM.com, online learning: *"Overcoming Self-Sabotage"* and *other courses.*

Deans M.D., Emily *"The Gut-Brain Connection, Mental Illness,* and *Disease"*, Psychobiotics, immunology, and *the theory of all chronic, Psychology Today* (posted 6 April 2014).

Dunn Buron, Kari (2007) *"A 5 is Against the Law!"*, AAPC Publishing.

Elrod, Hal (2016) *"The Miracle Morning"*, Hodder & Stoughton.

Ford, Debbie (2008) *"Why Good People do Bad Things: How to Stop Being Your Own Worst Enemy"*, HarperOne.

Giddens, Anthony (1992) *"The Transformation of Intimacy"*, Stanford University Press.

Goleman, Daniel (1996) *"Emotional Intelligence; Why it can matter more than IQ",* Bloomsbury Publishing PLC.

Hari, Johann (2018) *"Lost Connections"*, Bloomsbury Publishing.

Hugman, Richard (1991) *"Power in Caring Professions"*, Palgrave.

James, Oliver (2007) *"Affluenza"*, Vermilion.

Layne, Linda (2003) *"Motherhood Lost"*, Routledge & CRC Press.

LeDoux, Joseph (1999) *"The Emotional Brain: The Mysterious Underpinnings of Emotional Life"*, W&N.

Lindenfield, Gael (2000) *"Confident Children: help children feel good about themselves"*, HarperCollins.

Mental Health (First Aid) England, online training support.

Van Der Kolk, Bessel (2014) *"The Body Keeps the Score: Brain, Mind and Body in the Healing of Trauma"*, Penguin Random House.

Walker, Alice (1982) *"The Color Purple"*, Harcourt Brace Jovanovich.

Walter, Tony (1994) *"The Revival of Death"*, Routledge.

Wiseman, Sara *"Heal Your Family Karma"*, Kindle edition.

Useful organisations

Action for Elder Abuse	0808 808 8141
	(9am – 5pm, Monday to Friday)
	www.thenationalcareline.org
Angioma Alliance: because brains shouldn't bleed	www.angioma.org
Black Lives Matter	www.blacklivesmatter.com
Brain and Spine Foundation	0808 808 1000
	www.brainandspine.org.uk
British Legion	0808 802 8080
	(8am to 8pm, 7 days a week)
	www.britishlegion.org.uk
Cavernoma Alliance UK	01305 213876
	hello@cavernoma.org.uk
ChildLine	0800 1111 *(24 hour helpline)*
	www.childline.org.uk
Cruse Bereavement Care	0800 808 1677
	www.cruse.org.uk
Gamblers Anonymous	0330 094 0322
	www.gamblersanonymous.org.uk
Heads Together	www.headstogether.org.uk
Headway	0808 800 2244
	(9am – 5pm, Monday to Friday)
	www.headway.org.uk
Limbless Association	www.limbless-association.org
MHFA England online training support	0203 928 0760 www.mhfaengland.org

MIND	0300 123 3393
	(9am – 6pm) or text 86463
	www.mind.org.uk
National Centre for	0207 186 8270
Domestic Violence	0800 970 2070
	www.nationaldahelpline.org.uk
NSPCC	0808 800 5000
	(8am – 10pm Monday to Friday
	and 9am – 6pm at weekends)
	www.nspcc.org.uk
PTSD UK	www.ptsduk.org
Respect	0808 8010327
Men's Advice	www.respect.uk.net
Samaritans	116 123 *(24 hour helpline)*
	www.samaritans.org
Spinal Injuries Association	www.spinal.co.uk
The Good Grief Trust	www.thegoodgrieftrust.org
Victim Support	0808 168 9111 *(24 hour helpline)*
	www.victimsupport.org.uk
Young Carers	0300 123 1053
	www.carers.org

_____

Super healing quotes

_____

*"Loss is painful. It crushes hearts, steals dreams
and destroys relationships."*

Cruse Bereavement Care

*"One of the biggest mistakes we make is assuming
that other people think the way we think."*

Sonya Teclai

"Yesterday is heavy. Put it down."

Tinybuddha.com

*"I can tell who my safe people are because
I don't hold my breath when I'm around them.
I'm free to show up with all my feelings."*

Annecarlymm.com

*"Grief is not a straight line that disappears
into the horizon. It's a curvy line that goes up and
down, thins out for a while then widens
when you're unsuspecting."*

Cruse Bereavement Care

*"Sometimes the strength within you
is not a big fiery flame for all to see,
it is just a tiny spark that whispers ever so softly,
'You got this, keep going.' "*

www.littlenivi.com

*"Don't think of introversion as something
that needs to be cured."*

Susan Cain

"People start to heal the moment they feel heard."

Paul Boynton

*"We didn't understand as children that our parents
still had work to do on themselves."*

Maryam Hasnaa

*"We need to remember that a beautiful soul
is never forgotten."*

Cruse Bereavement Care

Facebook Cavernoma support groups

Here are some comments from my posts on the Facebook support groups, 'Cavernoma Alliance' UK and the 'Angioma Alliance for Cavernoma, Cavernous Malformation, Cavernous Angioma' Chicago:

"Mine is in the right parietal lobe and exactly the same symptoms as yours, nerve conductor studies normal but terrible tingling and neuropathy. I am only just diagnosed Wendy, so your thread is very reassuring to me. My immune system is rubbish so I am taking extra precautions and will continue to do so after 'normal' is resumed."

"I was told by my neuro that any neurological damage and symptoms make you more vulnerable. The article I read the other day describes if you have any type of neurological issues then you are at risk. Numbness, tingling, anything that makes a bleed more probable. I feel like my brain will explode with this tingling."

"We are working on a study at the Mayo Clinic and the University of Chicago to gather the up to date impact of the virus on all our patients."

"For most people, cavernoma is not like a chronic neurological disease such as.... but patients with cavernomas are impaired in a way similar to neurology patients...."

"I have been left with identical symptoms to yours, numbness, tingling, occasional electrical pain and weakness... every now and then I forget common words and produce word soup. Clearly, your symptoms are related to your cavernoma."

"Mine is in the right lobe and I get a lot of the same symptoms. As the group will tell you, not many understand cavernomas so it's hard for people to support you... I am going through ill health retirement with the local authority. They seem to think over time it will go away and I will get better."

"Please be reassured that what you are experiencing are common symptoms of cavernoma. Cavernomas are rare and the medical professionals sometimes give wrong information."

Health assessment

An independent assessor reviewed my medical notes, between April 2009 and May 2018.

Wendy first presented with symptoms of tingling hands in 2011. She has since presented with joint pain and stiffness in her ankles, knees, hips, lower back, hands, wrists and jaw. She complains of muscle weakness and loss of sensation with associated tingling, jangling and tremoring. She is tired and easily fatigued. She is being treated for hypothyroidism and low vitamin D levels. She is prone to respiratory tract infections, sinusitis and skin irritations. Wendy has experienced multiple miscarriages and a year of multiple bereavements. Wendy appears to have experienced an escalation in symptoms over the last three years leading to increasing concern for her health. Wendy's concerns appear to have been dismissed as anxiety on multiple occasions. Tests have been completed for Lupus, Lyme Disease, rheumatoid factor, a nerve conductor test but no comparison test over time considering increase in symptomology.

Current symptoms: numbness to upper lip, abnormal tongue movements, tongue shortened in length, quivering tongue sensation, tingling in lips and tongue, joint pain, muscle weakness, numbness and loss of sensation in peripheries, tingling in hands and feet, jangling, pulsating brain sensation, pain, stiffness, ache, worse on use and over the course of the day. Ankle swelling in evenings, tiredness and fatigue.

(Information based on summary of medical notes).

Family history of: heart attacks, cancer, sepsis, hypothyroidism, Myasthenia gravis, miscarriage, learning disability, cerebral palsy, leukaemia, embolism and high blood pressure.

Previous medical history of: seizures, multiple vasovagal attacks, dizzy spells, ankle problems, multiple miscarriages, wrist joint pain, chronic rhinitis and ear problems, eye twitching, blocked ears, headaches, abdominal pain, borderline APTT (m/c panel), knee symptoms, Eustachian tube dysfunction? Clotting screening test abnormal, autoimmune profile – normal, 2007 genetic testing requested by gynae (legacy attachment – outcome??) 2008 – High Serum TSH, L ovarian cyst – drained.

April 09	Monocyte count abnormal – mildly high.
April – June 09	Placenta has accessory lobe, ragged membranes on delivery. Abdominal pain. Scan – normal.
Oct 09	Faint symptoms, hip pain.
March 10	Hip pain.
April 10	Physio.
July 11	Low abdominal pains.
Aug 11	Pelvic pain.
Sept 11	Anteverted uterus – USS ovaries normal, no endometriosis seen.
Oct 11	Tingling sensation in fingers.
Sept 12	Ankle pain – aching and swollen – tested rheumatoid factor – normal.
Feb 14	Complaining of chest pain in evenings, ankle swelling in evenings.
Sept 14	Insomnia, irregular cycles.
Sept 14	Off sick with pain and upper respiratory tract infection.
May 15	Shortness of breath, tired, rapid heart rate at times, serum ferritin borderline.
Sept 15	Sebaceous cyst, sinusitis.
April 16	Abdominal pain – bloods normal.
May 16	Colposcopic biopsy cervix normal. Abdo pain – exclude coeliac – test required.

June 16	Peripheral neuropathy – tingling fingers, distribution not carpal tunnel, patient worried re MS (GP says most likely diagnosis: worries a lot).
July 16	Neurologist referral – GP writes 'peripheral neuropathy, patient still convinced something is wrong, lots of unrelated symptoms but patient thinks MS and under-active thyroid'.
Aug 16	Patient concerned re MS or MND.
Sept 16	Peripheral neuropathy – GP writes 'getting herself really worried, more minor symptoms'. Palpitations, pulse 60 bpm. Amitriptyline prescribed.
Sept 16	Peripheral neuropathy – sensations worse, c/o thyroid and muscles.
Oct 16	Serum TSH level – improved, nearly normal.
Oct 16	Peripheral neuropathy – no loss of power to hands. Rash.
Dec 16	Cyst, peripheral neuropathy, headaches, nerve tingling.
Jan 17	Seen by neurologist – no signs of pathology.
Jan 17	Nerve conduction studies – normal & EMG; no evidence of resting fasciculation potentials, myokymia, myotonia, neuromytonia, muscle cramp or tremor activity, no evidence to support radiculopathy or diffuse motor neuropathy.
Jan 17	Peripheral neuropathy, nortriptyline not helping. Patient wants MRI. GP thinks worry not helping.
March 17	Peripheral neuropathy – patient requesting scan.
March 17	Seen by neurologist .
April 17	Peripheral neuropathy – patient requested. repeat nerve conduction test. C/o hip pain, right side 3 weeks. No action taken. "She needs to stop worrying about it."

April 17	MRI scan normal.
April 17	Low back pain, likely muscular. Peripheral neuropathy – agreed to check magnesium levels.
April 17	Low back pain getting worse, difficulty getting in and out of car and turning. Straight leg raises painful. Painkillers prescribed. Magnesium level – normal.
May 17	Diagnosed with hypothyroidism, thyroxine started.
June 17	Serum TSH level – abnormal, Serum free T4 level – normal. Levothyroxine Sodium increased
June 17	Peripheral neuropathy; twitching, patient requested referral back to Neurology. GP advised to stop worrying about it.
Aug 17	Peripheral neuropathy; patient says symptoms worse, patient requested scan of hands.
Sept 17	Peripheral neuropathy – bumps on wrists, noticeable on hyperextension. GP says normal tissue that is more prominent.
Oct 17	Peripheral neuropathy.
Nov 17	Jaw pain – ongoing for some time, dull ache, top of both jaws, right and left. No abnormality identified within mouth.
Nov 17	Seen by neurologist.
Nov 17	Upper respiratory tract infection.
Jan 18	Upper respiratory tract infection, continues to get fasciculations to palm.
Jan 18	Peripheral neuropathy, twitching and numbness in hands, weakness and stiffness in feet, painful hips. Vitamin D level – low.

Jan 18	hbA1c – normal, Lyme disease igG – normal, Borrelia Burgdirferi – normal, Lupus screen normal. Prescription of vitamin D.
Feb 18	Ankle pain, skin irritation.
March 18	BP raised 160/100.
March 18	Seen by private neurologist – no evidence of neuro problems but no new tests conducted, diagnosis 'ill health anxiety'.
April 18	Peripheral neuropathy – c/o tingling in lips and tongue, serum calcium level – normal, serum cortisol level – normal, Serum CRP level – normal.
May 18	Nerve pain in jaw, skin irritation, tongue shortened in shape, quivering and scalloped at edges. On examination, no evidence of abnormality on tongue.
May 18	Neuro referral to hospital. Complaining of numbness to upper lip, abnormal tongue movements. GP says can't see new symptom.

August 2020 update

Physical wellbeing

The following physical symptoms remain:
constant altered sensation, touch deficit to finger tips, tingling and stiffness to hands, which significantly affects day-to-day life. My ankles are still an issue; they have improved but are still bothersome. My feet and hands can only be in water for 20 minutes before feeling unmanageably aggravated. I experience head buzzing, neck tingling, night headaches, instant thunderclap headaches, extended headaches, fleeting feelings of sadness (I presented with 8/10 pre-dispositions for

suicide, whilst undertaking recent suicide awareness training). I have word muddling (I think of the word then a similar word comes out) and brain fog. I'm medicated for high blood pressure, low vitamin D, night tingling and low folate/thyroid. I have sleep disturbance, insomnia, night time over-thinking and restlessness. I still faint easily if intoxicated or flying or walking at high altitude.

In terms of wellbeing, I have lost weight and I abstain from alcohol from January to October.

Emotional wellbeing

I am happy much of the time but have sweeping instances of mental sadness, which I feel physically, and which pass after a moment. They come from nowhere. As an individual, I am self-aware, self-assured, self-confident and humorous. At times, I 'over think' and can feel rejected, awkward, abandoned, left out, misunderstood and irritated. I am shy and sometimes solitary, even though I am well-loved, respected and socially integrated. I think about my bereavements daily but I do not feel overwhelmed by them. Emotionally, I feel I am healed as much as I am going to be. I do feel a genuine sense of self-purpose and a strong resolve 'to keep going' and to keep fighting my feelings from within. I channel this into living my best life, whenever I can, living ecologically and being a good person.

Occupational health retirement report and magnetic resonance imaging (MRIs)

This report, dated 19th May 2020, is based on the following documentation:

- History taken at the assessment
- Your referral and the job description/person specification
- The previous occupational health report dated 9th December 2019
- Copy of specialist report dated 1st April 2020 from Consultant Neurologist

I consider the information I have available sufficient upon which to base a clear opinion for the purpose of ill health retirement.

Summary of Employment History

Mrs Wren is employed as an Assistant Team Manager. She is required to be able to drive and the work includes a leadership role. The role required both administrative work and a requirement for home visits. She has been in the role for approximately 20 years and she usually works three days per week.

Summary of Medical Information

Mrs Wren has been suffering from altered sensation in her limbs since December 2015 after developing stomach pain. She initially felt as if there were electric currents in her upper and lower limbs which subsequently reduced, and she is now left with altered sensation. She was initially referred to Neurology for investigation with a negative nerve conduction studies and MRI scan. She has had a second MRI scan which has confirmed a 6mm intercranial cavernoma. She also has a degree of cervical spondylosis. Mrs Wren's neurologist did not feel that the cavernoma was resulting in clinical symptoms, although these can on occasion cause neurological problems. The cervical spondylosis may result in some arm symptoms which can be treated with nerve root injections.

Mrs Wren's neurologist has diagnosed her with Functional Neurological Disorder, which Mrs Wren disputes. She is waiting for further investigation which will include another set of nerve conduction studies. Having reviewed the symptoms of Functional Neurological Disorder, the symptoms that Mrs Wren describes could be explained by this condition with dysfunction of her nervous system resulting in altered sensation and muscle twitching if no other abnormality is found on investigation.

Treatment for Functional Neurological Disorder is based on the symptoms experienced, with physiotherapy for movement disorders and psychological therapy and occupational therapy to help address the impact of the condition on the individual's life. No specific medication is recommended for the condition.

In considering the results to date, although Mrs Wren will undergo a second set of nerve conduction studies, this is unlikely to change the current clinical picture and this report is based on the functional capacity which is impacting on Mrs Wren, rather than a specific diagnosis. She is taking medication and has accessed acupuncture which has not provided any substantial improvement with her symptoms. Although therapy, including injection therapy for the cervical spondylosis and physiotherapy for the twitching might be helpful, it is unlikely that any known management to date will have a significant impact on the current sensory symptoms.

Details of Functional Capacity

Mrs Wren is suffering from altered sensation in her hands and feet. She struggles with grip of her hands and has had difficulty typing which triggers her sensory symptoms. She is right-handed and her symptoms are worse on the right. Although voice-activated software might help to some extent, there would still be the need for some keyboard use. She is limited in her walking and finds her knees are stiff and twitch regularly. She also has muscle twitches in her neck and head which affects her sleeping. She manages to undertake some household tasks, but she needs her husband's help with cooking and he undertakes the hoovering. She struggles with lifting anything heavy. She has also found difficulty in driving, which is a key requirement for her role.

Mrs Wren has tried to reduce her hours at work, but she found being at work three days per week was resulting in symptoms worsening at the end of the day and she was unable to sustain even these reduced hours. Her symptoms have not shown any improvement since stopping work and she continues to be significantly impacted, despite managing her activity appropriately. On the balance of probabilities, even with further investigation and consideration of specific management for her symptoms, it is unlikely that there will be sufficient improvement for a return to her substantive role to be achievable prior to her retirement age. Considering the current symptoms and impact these are having on day to day activities, I do not consider Mrs Wren to be able to undertake gainful employment as defined in the regulations. If her symptoms do show some improvement with treatment, she may in due course be able to do some part-time work, but as stated above, I do not believe this will meet the criteria for gainful employment.

Recommendations

The ill health retirement application is made under the Local Government Pension Scheme Regulations 2013.

I have therefore concluded that the individual is suffering from a condition, that more likely than not, renders her permanently incapable of discharging efficiently the duties of her employment with this employer because of ill health.

I can confirm that the employee is not immediately capable of undertaking any gainful employment and it is unlikely that the employee will be capable of undertaking any gainful employment before her normal pension age.

I have included a completed ill health certificate which reflects my opinion. I have attached a copy of my full report and I CERTIFY THAT:

I have not previously advised, or given an opinion on, or been involved in this case;

AND

I am not acting, and have not at any time acted, as the representative of the person named in part A of the application form, the employer, or any other party in relation to this case;

AND

I am registered with the General Medical Council

AND

I am a Fellow of the Faculty of Occupational Medicine ©

MRI Scans

The following MRI scans of my head and neck, taken on 7th March 2020, demonstrate my 'inactive' cavernoma, which is located in my right parietal lobe.

My opinion is that they do have some effect on the following: my intolerance to alcohol, my inability to fly without feeling faint and my night time and general headaches. I also muddle my words, so I cognitively think of a word but a very similar word is spoken. For example, house becomes bungalow, two words merge into one and/or I am just aware that something has come out slightly wrong.

This is a neurological symptom that I am able to quickly perceive in others. This, and my early disrupted neural pathways, may also partly explain my high levels of perception and my sharp self-awareness, self-confidence and self-assurance. And, perhaps also, my auras and unexplained experiences, such as 'presence' and out of body experiences, which have occurred around dying, bereavement and loss.

Scan 1

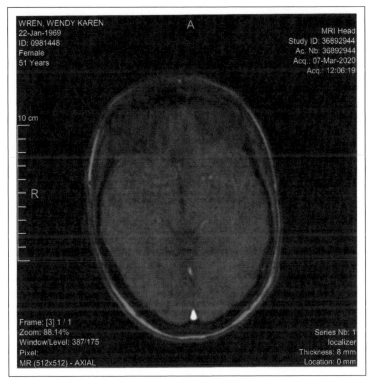

Scan 2

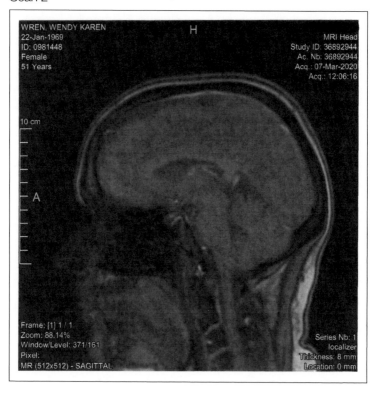

Scan 3

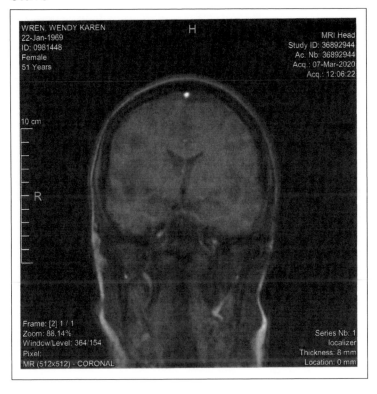

Scan 4

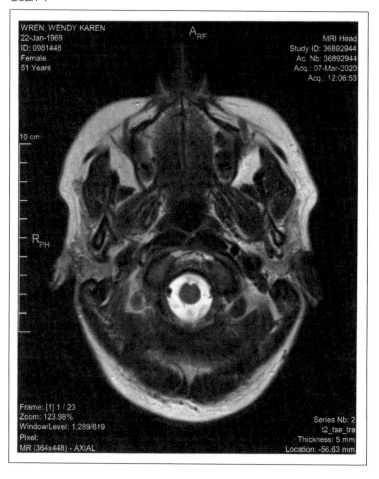

Scan 5

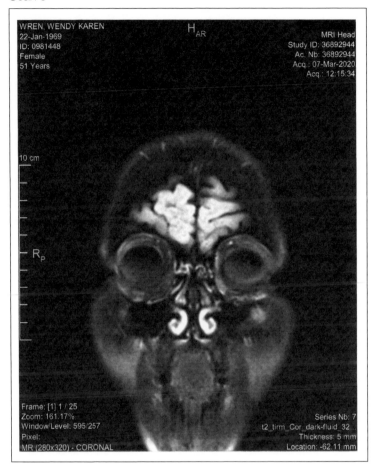

Surviving a 'New Norm'

Chronology of my bereavements

I was born on 22nd January 1969.

Prior trauma 1943	My father's mother dies, when he is six years old.
Prior trauma 1950	My father's sister dies, at 11 years of age, from leukaemia.
Prior trauma 1961	My brother dies, still birth.
Prior trauma 1966	My father's other sister dies, from an embolism, aged 30.
1968	My mother's father dies from suicide. He is found floating in the lake, at the Royal Military Academy, Camberley, with sleeping tablets in his stomach, on autopsy. My mother's contraceptive pill fails, as she was constantly being sick and I am conceived.
1969	My mother's mother dies in hospital, 'broken heart', lungs and chest.
1982	My father's father dies, heart attack.
1985	My school friend Dean takes his own life.
1990	First terrorist incident in Cairo, Egypt (sisters Yonnie and Pam present with me).
1996	My university friend dies, swollen brain, no further information provided to us.
1997	Second terrorist incident in Luxor/Aswan, Egypt (Steve, sister Yonnie and Peter, my brother-in-law, present with me).
1998	I had bereavement counselling at university.

Chronology of my bereavements

Sept 2001	My miscarriage of twins.
Nov 2001	My father dies of a heart attack, my husband and I attempt to resuscitate him, before the ambulance arrives.
2001	Two of Steve's uncles die of old age, Len and Maurice (who was an uncle figure, Esme's partner).
2001 Dec	Steve's father dies of a heart attack, complicated by lung disease.
2003	I had more bereavement therapy with a clinical psychologist.
2003 – 2008	Multiple miscarriages.
2007	Steve's Uncle Arthur dies.
2009	Julie Harrison and her daughter are murdered by her ex-partner, he then shoots himself.
2012	School friend John dies, from drug complications. He had lost his leg and had ongoing health problems.
2016	Nana Joyce dies of old age.
2016	School friend Martin dies of a heart attack.
2016	Aunt Esme dies of old age.
2016	Diane, school mum/friend dies, late diagnosed cancer.
2018	School friend Katherine dies, cancer.
2019	Wilko, basketball/school dad dies, face cancer.

| 2020 | Steve's cousin Dave dies, heart attack, not related to Covid-19. |
| 2020 | School friend Wayne dies, heart attack. |

Please can I apologise for anyone else I may have left out as I have only recorded the deaths that I have needed to process.

Bereavement anniversaries

My most significant bereavements have occurred between September and December. This coincides with the sun 'dimming' and the rain becoming more prominent. To block out the grey clouds which invade my brain, I walk and walk and walk. I have even (reluctantly) converted myself to 'enjoying' jogging. To say I'm a convert is a slight exaggeration, but taking one step at a time perhaps best symbolises the path to healing. The autumnal days also make me focus on actively using my electric head and back massager and Ted, my 'sun lamp'.

Around Christmas time (not necessarily Christmas Day itself) I ritually take a wreath or stone ornament and visit my father's grave. My father and I have a 'catch up' – I think you can behave in any such way at cemeteries. It is a very specific space to grieve where people are generally understanding, flexible, compassionate and respectful. People often interact closely at these places, I guess given the acknowledgment of shared feelings. On one occasion, a middle-aged man, who I'd never met, came over and gave me a hug and then walked away, no words. Touch is a powerful way to connect as compassionate human beings.

Whilst visiting my father's cemetery, I say a little hello on behalf of a school friend, to her first baby, who is buried at the same cemetery. Sometimes on the same day, I visit other cemeteries nearby and places where ashes have been scattered. It's a healing and peaceful thing to do and takes me out of the commercial rush around Christmas-time commitments.

Bereavement anniversaries are a reminder of both our loss(es) and also our happy or sad times. Sometimes I forget some anniversaries, only to guiltily remember them a few days later. Anniversaries can, without doubt, bring about a myriad of feelings, both mental and physical. Feelings can range from physical devastation to indifference. Sometimes such anniversaries can bring to the forefront a delayed grief reaction. This has happened to me where, at the moment of the loss, I have been consumed by a previous loss, registering a death, arranging a funeral or just trying to function competently and effectively.

Personal losses leading up to bereavement anniversaries are unique to every individual and if it's helpful, they can be commiserated, spontaneously or planned, in the following ways: visiting the grave of your loved one, attending the crematorium, visiting a National Trust or similar establishment, going to a place where their ashes are scattered or a tree is planted, enjoying the day chatting with a close friend, journaling, shutting out the world with a 'duvet day', bathing in a particular scent, writing a letter to the person you have lost, having a glass of their favourite beverage, painting, phoning a helpline, visiting someone who makes you laugh... the list is endless. It very much depends on the individual and how they seek comfort.

_____

About the author

_____

Wendy Wren grew up in Frogmore, on the borders of Hampshire and Surrey. She was the youngest of four children, born to an understandably anxious mother (whose father had taken his own life the year before Wendy was born) and a father who had bereavement and trauma issues, having lost his mother and both sisters at a young age.

During her childhood, Wendy was run over and burnt by a car, impaled on a tree whilst climbing, fell through a frozen lake whilst ice-skating and almost choked on a scud missile-type gobstopper. She always joked though that her biggest risk was from her mother's cooking!

During her teenage years, Wendy and her sister, Pam, were persistent shoplifters and, along with her best friend, Kay, they 'grounded' a local airport, whilst playing a game of chicken, which was later described as 'causing an international incident'. People who know the family are amazed that, not only did the children survive, but they became fairly well-functioning adults!

On leaving home at 18, Wendy moved into a house with a convicted fraudster, only to realise the gravity of his criminal nature eight years later, when she received a bill for £44,000 for mortgage fraud. Thankfully, the investigation into Wendy's involvement was finally dropped. At 19, Wendy asked her parents if she could move back in to the family home but the emotional pressures of her brother's learning disabilities were too much to cope with. As a result, Wendy and her sister, Pam, found themselves homeless and spent six months living in a tent, close to Brighton, where they both worked for nursing agencies, saving up the deposit to rent a flat. Wendy's eldest sister, Yvonne (known as Yonnie), also moved in and subsequently, in the local care home circles, the girls were fondly known as 'The Goddard Sisters'!

After a few years of living in Brighton, Wendy met her husband, Steve, who pretty much 'rescued' her and gave her somewhere suitable to live. They have since lived in Hook, London, Bulford,

Whitchurch, Hartley Wintney and Portreath. Wendy went on to study a BA (Honours) degree in Sociology and Criminology, a Masters and Diploma in Social Work, a Practice Teaching Award and a PTLLS (Preparing to Teach in the Lifelong Learning Sector) qualification. She has also studied and worked in the beauty and calligraphy industries.

Professionally, in a social work context, Wendy worked with traumatised children in the youth justice system for 15 years, later including criminal profiling. She also worked as a support tutor at Royal Holloway University of London and spent several years in Fostering Management. This role involved leading on business continuity with regard to potential major incidents, terrorist attacks, pandemic response and special evacuation. Wendy says she learnt most about morality and loyalty from working with young offenders. She currently contributes as a volunteer for 'Cruse Bereavement Care' and 'Volunteer Cornwall'.

Wendy herself has experienced many bereavements, from illnesses to incidents including suicides, a double murder, miscarriages and early deaths. Wendy has a 6mm brain cavernoma in her right parietal lobe and a Functional Neurological Disorder.

Wendy has two wonderful rays of sunshine, her children, Max and Ruby-Rose. The family now live between Hampshire and Portreath, Cornwall, where Wendy spends her time writing, volunteering and walking her dog on the North Cornwall coast.

————————

"As long as you feel pain,
you're still alive.
As long as you make mistakes,
you're still human.
And as long as you keep trying,
there's still hope."

Susan Gale

————————

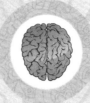